"This is a really clear, compelling, understanding, and engaging response to the biggest objections people have to Christianity today. Read it, wrestle with it, and see what your friends make of it."

Sam Allberry, speaker; author, *Why Does God Care Who I Sleep With?* and *7 Myths about Singleness*

"Rebecca McLaughlin doesn't shy away from difficult conversations about heaven, hell, sexuality, and racism but handles them with gentleness, humility, and a refreshing humor that teens will appreciate. Best of all, she presents the gospel so clearly and beautifully. I'm thankful for this winsome resource that I can recommend to young Christians and non-Christians alike."

Quina Aragon, spoken-word artist; author, *Love Made: A Story of God's Overflowing, Creative Heart* and *Love Gave: A Story of God's Greatest Gift*

"Young people might not always articulate their questions about life. But they are wondering. *10 Questions Every Teen Should Ask (and Answer) about Christianity* can help them both express and satisfy their emerging questions and longings. We wish we'd had this book when we were raising our children! But now we can give it away—confidently—starting with our own grandchildren."

Ray and Jani Ortlund, President and Executive Vice President, Renewal Ministries

"*10 Questions Every Teen Should Ask (and Answer) about Christianity* is the book every parent, teacher, youth worker, and young person has been waiting for. In her down-to-earth, relatable, winsome, and brilliant manner, Rebecca McLaughlin tackles the major questions confronting this generation, showing that Jesus is still the answer to our greatest needs and longings. If we don't want to lose a generation, we must have the courage to wrestle with hard questions and show that Christianity is relevant in our rapidly changing world."

Christine Caine, Founder, A21 and Propel Women

T0054277

"Our world is complex. Growing up today and having to confront that complexity is not easy. In this short book, McLaughlin helps young adolescents confront, understand, and interpret the complexity of our world in continual dialogue with the central claims of the Christian faith. Readers will have their minds challenged and illuminated; by struggling through these issues, they will be brought closer to the truth."

Tyler J. VanderWeele, John L. Loeb and Frances Lehman Loeb Professor of Epidemiology, Harvard University

"As a father of five, I was so excited to know about this book. My excitement only grew as I read the truths Rebecca McLaughlin engages in such an accessible manner—many references to Harry Potter and Disney films! Most of all, I was excited to have a theologically rich book that deals with challenging questions that I could place in the hands of my children. This is such an important tool to disciple the next generation!"

John Perritt, Director of Resources, Reformed Youth Ministries

10 Questions Every Teen Should Ask

(and Answer) about Christianity

10 Questions
Every Teen Should Ask
(and Answer)
about Christianity

REBECCA McLAUGHLIN

:: CROSSWAY®

WHEATON, ILLINOIS

Trade paperback ISBN: 978-1-4335-7166-4
ePub ISBN: 978-1-4335-7169-5
PDF ISBN: 978-1-4335-7167-1
Mobipocket ISBN: 978-1-4335-7168-8

Library of Congress Cataloging-in-Publication Data

Names: McLaughlin, Rebecca, 1980- author.
Title: 10 questions every teen should ask (and answer) about Christianity / Rebecca McLaughlin.
Other titles: Ten questions every teen should ask (and answer) about Christianity
Description: Wheaton, Illinois : Crossway, 2021.
Identifiers: LCCN 2020020314 (print) I LCCN 2020020315 (ebook) I ISBN 9781433571664 (trade paperback) I ISBN 9781433571671 (pdf) I ISBN 9781433571688 (mobi) I ISBN 9781433571695 (epub)
Subjects: LCSH: Christianity—Juvenile literature.
Classification: LCC BR125.5 .M45 2021 (print) I LCC BR125.5 (ebook) I DDC 239—dc23
LC record available at https://lccn.loc.gov/2020020314
LC ebook record available at https://lccn.loc.gov/2020020315

Crossway is a publishing ministry of Good News Publishers.

LSC   30   29   28   27   26   25   24   23
15   14   13   12   11   10   9   8   7   6

For Miranda, Eliza, and Luke,
who ask the hardest questions,
and for everyone who wonders
what this strange world
is all about.

Contents

Preface 11

Note to Parents, Grandparents, Guardians, and Friends 13

Introduction 19

1 How Can I Live My Best Life Now? 27
Mental and Physical Health Benefits of the Christian Life

2 Isn't Christianity against Diversity? 41
Racism / Slavery / Christianity as the Most Diverse Movement in History

3 Can Jesus Be True for You but Not for Me? 55
Universal Truth / Relativism / Evangelism

4 Can't We Just Be Good without God? 67
God as the Basis for Morality / 9/11 / Hitler / Stalin / Human Identity / Abortion

5 **How Can You Believe the Bible Is True?** 83

Evidence for the Gospels / Evidence for the Resurrection /
True versus Literal

6 **Hasn't Science Disproved Christianity?** 97

Origins of Science / Science and Faith Controversies /
Christian Scientists Today

7 **Why Can't We Just Agree That Love Is Love?** 113

Marriage / Sex / Singleness / Friendship / Same-Sex Attraction /
Pornography / Abuse

8 **Who Cares If You're a Boy or a Girl?** 135

Gender / Feminism / Transgender and Non-Binary Identities

9 **Does God Care When We Hurt?** 157

God's Sovereignty in Suffering / God's Care for Us / Prayer /
Purpose

10 **How Can You Believe in Heaven and Hell?** 169

Meaning of Heaven and Hell / Sin and Judgment /
Salvation / Invitation

A "Thank You" Note 183

Notes 187

General Index 197

Scripture Index 203

Preface

When I was a kid, I wanted to be a poet. But my first book wasn't a gathering of poems. It was a gathering of ideas from some of the world's brainiest people. After nine years of talking with professors at top universities, I felt like I had a roadmap of objections to Christianity, showing where the dead ends lay and pointing to the highways. *Confronting Christianity: 12 Hard Questions for the World's Largest Religion* (Crossway, 2019) is that map. It looks at twelve reasons *not* to believe in Jesus and argues that—if we look at them more closely—they stop being roadblocks and instead become signposts.

I was thrilled when *Confronting Christianity* was featured as one of the only books about faith on the *TED Talks* Summer Reading List and named Christian Book of the Year 2020 by *Christianity Today* magazine. But I was most thankful for the readers who let me know how much the book meant to them as they'd examined their own beliefs or answered questions from exploring friends. As I read these messages, it struck me that kids and teens have complex questions too. In fact, in my experience, kids ask the hardest questions of all.

You could say this book is a simplified version of *Confronting Christianity*. In one sense, it is. I've written it for folks who aren't yet ready to drive, so they don't need quite so extensive a map. But navigating on a bike has its own challenges, and I believe in taking the training wheels off as soon as possible and letting people explore for themselves.

If you're ready to drive, you may be ready for *Confronting Christianity*. That book gives all the footnotes for the claims I make in this book and explores some issues not included here. If you're not yet driving age, but you have real questions about the world in which we live, this book is for you.

Rebecca McLaughlin

October 2020

Note to Parents, Grandparents, Guardians, and Friends

I finally gave up Christianity when I was 15," wrote famous atheist Richard Dawkins in his latest book, *Outgrowing God: A Beginner's Guide* (2019).[1] Dawkins hoped to reach the rising generation of kids with the good news that they don't need religion. In the decades since the New Atheist movement launched, you might think this was the only message sounding from the academic world. But that is simply not the case.

Religious belief was supposed to decline as modernization swept the world.[2] But it hasn't. Being a world-class academic and a serious, orthodox Christian was supposed to be increasingly untenable. But it isn't. Giving up on religion was supposed to make people happier, healthier, and more moral. But it doesn't.[3] In fact, even Richard Dawkins has had to acknowledge (grudgingly) the evidence that people who believe in God seem to behave better than those who don't. He thinks it rather patronizing to say, "Of course you and I are too intelligent to believe in God, but we think it would be a good idea if *other* people did!"[4] And yet that does seem to be where the evidence points. Broadly speaking, religious belief and practice seem to be good for society—and good for kids. Writing in the *Wall Street Journal* in 2019, therapist Erica Komisar gave this provocative advice: "Don't believe in God? Lie to your children."[5]

Komisar was not shooting in the dark. Mirroring the mental and physical health benefits for adults, there is a growing body of evidence that regular religious practice is measurably good for the health, happiness, and pro-social behavior of our kids. In the same year that Dawkins released his book, the Harvard School of Public Health published the results of a longitudinal study on the impact of a religious upbringing on adolescents and found that it contributes to a wide range of health and well-being outcomes later in life.[6] In an op-ed for *USA Today*, Harvard professor of epidemiology Tyler VanderWeele summarized some of the key findings:

- Children who were raised in a religious or spiritual environment were better protected from the "big three" dangers of adolescence: depression, drugs, and risky sexual behaviors.
- Those who attended religious services regularly were subsequently 12 percent less likely to have high depressive symptoms and 33 percent less likely to use illicit drugs.
- Those who prayed or meditated frequently were 30 percent less likely to start having sex at a young age and 40 percent less likely to have a sexually transmitted disease.
- Moreover, children with a religious upbringing were also more likely to subsequently have higher levels of happiness, of a sense of purpose, of volunteering, and of forgiveness of others.[7]

Of course, these studies do not mean that belief in God is right, or that Christianity is true. It should, however, give us pause before dismissing religious perspectives out of hand and assuming that our kids are just better off without. As Erika Komisar put it,

> As a therapist, I'm often asked to explain why depression and anxiety are so common among children and adolescents. One of the most important explanations—and perhaps the most neglected—is declining interest in religion.[8]

If this data is challenging for non-religious parents, the "declining interest in religion" (at least in the West) is worrying for believers. Just as evidence for the benefits of religious upbringing is mounting, cultural tides are pulling kids and teens away from religious moorings. So what are parents, grandparents, and carers on all sides of these great debates to do?

Whatever our beliefs about God, there are some things on which I'm sure we agree: we all want our kids to be happy, healthy, purpose-filled, and good. Few of us would want to lie to our kids, especially about our deepest beliefs. We want them to know the truth. But we also want to protect them from plausible-sounding lies. Deep down we know there's a tension: to keep our kids truly safe in the long run, we must let them risk-take now. We know this when it comes to practical skills. A baby won't learn to walk unless we let him fall. A child won't learn to ride a bike unless we let her risk a tumble or two. The teenager who wasn't trusted with a bike won't be ready for a car. So how does this translate to the realm of ideas?

For some parents, protecting their kids from dangerous ideas feels like a must. I've heard this both from Christians who don't want their kids exposed to atheism, and from atheists who don't want their kids exposed to Christianity. I've even heard it from parents who think they are very open-mindedly encouraging their kids to explore different religious traditions, while insisting they respect each tradition equally. For these folks, the dangerous idea is that one religion might actually be *true*. Many of us who are now in the thick of parenting were raised with the idea that questioning someone's religious beliefs was arrogant, offensive, and wrong. Beliefs were personal and should not be challenged.

In this book, I want to offer a different approach. Rather than protecting my kids from divergent ideas, or urging them to affirm all beliefs equally, I want to equip them to have real conversations with real people who really think differently from them—and from me. I want them to learn how to listen well and how to question what they hear. If what I believe is true, it will stand up to scrutiny.

The Christian faith sprang up in a world that was violently hostile to its claims. But rather than extinguishing the small spark of the early church, the winds of opposition gave it oxygen to spread. Two thousand years later (as I explain in chapter 1) it's still spreading. But I don't want my kids to believe in Jesus just because I say so, or just because it's the largest and most diverse religion in the world, or just because going to church makes you happier, healthier, and more generous to others. I want them to see Jesus for themselves and to believe that what he says about himself is true.

Wanting this for my kids doesn't mean hiding other options. If anything, I believe Jesus shines more brightly when all the veils are stripped away. My guess is that if you're not a follower of Jesus, you also have enough confidence in your beliefs to think they'll stand up to scrutiny, and that you too would like the young people you love—as a parent, grandparent, uncle, aunt, or friend—to think for themselves. My hope is that this book will challenge every reader to do just that. And, in order to do so, we're going to have some adult conversations.

This book engages with some big ideas. It talks about racism and slavery, marriage and sexuality, gender and transgender questions, abortion and pornography, 9/11, Hitler, Stalin, heaven, and hell. In it, I share my early and ongoing experience of same-sex attraction, and the story of one of my best friends, who had multiple sexual relationships with other girls before becoming a Christian as an undergrad at Yale. Whatever your child's current beliefs or emerging attractions, I hope this book will be a help to them. I've tried to write with empathy and care.

My eldest child has just turned ten, and I've written the book in a way I'd be comfortable for her to read. But kids develop at very different rates, and you'll be the best judge of your own child's readiness. You may want to read the book first yourself before passing it on to your kids. You may want to read it *with* the children you love. Or you may think they'll prefer to read for themselves. In any case, my hope is that it will prompt fruitful conversations.

If you are not a Christian, I hope this book will at least give your child a handle on some of the best Christian thinking from some of the most credible sources, when too often we only hear in public from the worst. If you do consider yourself a follower of Jesus, I hope it will encourage your child to take the claims of Christ very seriously, and not to be afraid to ask hard questions.

I'm currently reading the Harry Potter series to my kids, and I must warn you that this book is full of Harry Potter spoilers! If you're a J. K. Rowling fan and the young person you love hasn't yet read her books, you might want to hold off sharing this book for now. If your children aren't ready for the entire Harry Potter series, they may not be ready for this book either.

Harry Potter was eleven when he found out there was magic in the world. Richard Dawkins would say that believing in the Christian story is about as childish as believing that Harry Potter's world is true. But the thousands of Christian professors at the top of their fields—ranging from physics to philosophy to psychology to epidemiology—would disagree. My hope is that this book will help young people to start thinking for themselves. That's one point on which Dawkins and I agree.

Introduction

In *Harry Potter and the Prisoner of Azkaban*, Harry has just run away from his awful aunt and uncle's house when he sees an ominous black dog. He's rescued by the Knight Bus, which picks up stranded magical folk. But throughout the book, this dog keeps cropping up. Harry sees it in the tea leaves in Professor Trelawney's divination class. He sees it in the grounds of Hogwarts School. He even sees it in the bleachers of the Quidditch field. He's not sure if he's going mad, imagining this creature everywhere. But then one night it grabs his best friend Ron by the leg and drags him down a tunnel. Harry dashes after, terrified. At the end of the tunnel, he finds Ron in a haunted house. But the dog has gone. It's turned into the evil murderer Sirius Black, who betrayed Harry's parents to their deaths. Now he's going to murder Harry too.

Or so Harry thinks.

If you've read the Harry Potter books, you'll know that that's not right at all. Rather than trying to murder Harry, Sirius wants to protect him. Rather than betraying Harry's parents, Sirius was himself betrayed. Rather than being Harry's enemy, Sirius turns out to be his faithful friend. In fact, he's the closest thing to family Harry's got. When Harry first saw Sirius, all the evidence was against him. But when he found out the truth of who Sirius was, Harry's mind was changed. So was his heart.

When people look at Christianity, they sometimes make the same mistake that Harry made with Sirius. Many of my friends think Christianity is *against* the things they care about the most. My friends care about racial justice. They see the ways in which Christians have engaged in slavery and racism and they assume that Christianity is against racial justice. My friends hear Christians saying that Jesus is the only way to God, and they think this is arrogant and offensive to those who were raised with other religious beliefs. My friends think people should be able to date and marry whomever they want, but Christianity says that it's not okay to marry someone of the same sex. My friends are excited by the discoveries of science, and they think that believing in a Creator God is the opposite of believing in science. My friends believe that women are equal to men, and they think Christianity puts women down. My friends see all the pain and suffering in the world, and they think there couldn't possibly be a loving God in charge. But just as Harry's view of Sirius totally changed when he discovered more, when we look more closely at each of these concerns, our view of Christianity might just change as well.

Perhaps someone gave you this book, and you think believing in Jesus is dumb. When one of my best friends was a teenager, that's what she thought too. Rachel was *really* smart. The Christians she knew were not. Rachel liked her freedom: freedom to party, freedom to get drunk, freedom to try out different kinds of romantic relationships. She thought it was stupid to be a Christian, partly because you'd have to be dumb to believe the things Christians believe, and partly because you'd have to be dumb to follow a religion that stopped you from having fun. God totally changed Rachel's mind when she was in college. (I'll tell you more of her story in chapter 7.) If you're reading this book and you think like Rachel did, I'm really glad you're here. I hope you find these questions interesting and that they help you think more for yourself.

Maybe you're more like I was at your age. I remember feeling sure about following Jesus when I was nine years old. Most of my friends growing up thought being a Christian was weird, but I mostly didn't mind being different. At my school, being different was okay. (One girl wore wings to school every day for a year and no one cared!) But sometimes it was hard to disagree with all my friends. They thought the Bible was just made-up stories. They thought all religions were equally true. They thought Christians hated gay people and that Christians didn't think women were equal to men. Believing that some guy died on a cross and came back to life two thousand years ago so that we could be forgiven by God sounded crazy to them. Most of the teachers agreed. So were they right?

Since I was your age, I've spent a *really* long time studying, and I've met a lot of *ridiculously* smart people, including professors at some of the best universities in the world. Some of them think it's stupid to believe in Jesus. Others think that following Jesus is the cleverest thing we could possibly do, and that without Jesus, there is no meaning for our lives and no hope for our world. These people have lots of different stories of how they came to believe in Jesus. Some grew up in Christian families. Some became Christians as teenagers. Others started following Jesus when they were adults, because they realized Jesus was the answer to their biggest questions. And they're not alone. It's easy to imagine Christianity as old-fashioned and dying out, but there are actually more Christians in the world today than ever before.

When I was growing up, experts predicted that as the world became more modern, more educated, and more scientific, religious belief would naturally decline. But they were wrong. In Western countries, like England (where I'm from) and America (where I now live), the number of people who believe in God has decreased. But in the rest of the world, belief in God is actually *increasing*, and Christianity is still the most popular religion. In fact, there are *twice* as many people in the world who say they are Christians as there are who say they aren't religious.[1]

By the time you're my age, the percentage of people in the world who say they *don't* believe in God is likely to go down, while the percentage of people who say they are Christians is likely to go up. China is the largest country in the world. It is officially "atheist" (which means being sure that God doesn't exist). People in China can even be sent to prison for following Jesus. But the church in China is growing so fast that by 2025, there will likely be more Christians in China than in America, and some experts think that by 2060, more than half the people in China will be Christians![2]

Just because lots of people believe something doesn't make it right. Each of us must think carefully for ourselves about what we believe. But if you think that Christianity is dying out or that all the really educated people have stopped following Jesus, you might want to look more closely. Harvard professor Tyler Vander-Weele (whom you'll meet in chapter 1) says that—in light of all the evidence for Christianity—any educated person should look carefully at the claims of Jesus and be able to explain why he or she does or doesn't believe them.

The most important book to read if you want to know more about Jesus is the Bible. The Bible is the best-selling book of all time. Like the Harry Potter series, it tells one overarching story, but it's broken up into many shorter books (sixty-six in total!). But unlike the Harry Potter series, it claims to offer us the key to everlasting life. The Bible was written by many different human authors, but Christians believe that each of these human authors was inspired by God and that we can meet God and get to know him through this book. I'll reference the Bible at many points in this book, but if you're not familiar with the Bible, don't worry. I'll always explain what I'm talking about.

The Bible is divided into two parts. The first part is known as the Old Testament. This part of the Bible is shared by Jews and Christians. It tells us the story of God and his people before Jesus was born. The second part is called the New Testament. The New Testament tells us the story of Jesus's life, death, and resurrection in the four Gospels of Matthew, Mark, Luke, and John. It then tells the story of the early Christian movement in the book of Acts, and we get to read letters written by some of the first Christian leaders to some of the first Christian churches.

The Bible has done more to change the world than any book in history. In chapter 5, we'll look more closely at why we might think that the Bible is actually true. My hope is that—whether you already believe in Jesus or not—this book will make you want to read the Bible for yourself. You see, the Bible is a bit like an ancient treasure chest. Open it up, and you will find amazing riches with the power to change your life forever. But sometimes treasure chests get buried, and we need to dig through the dirt to find them. My hope is that this book will give you a shovel to dig through the ideas that sometimes stop people from wanting to read the Bible at all. But in order to read this book, I need you to take a risk.

To find out who Sirius really was, Harry had to dive down a tunnel. To read this book, and to understand Christianity, you need to dive in with an open mind. If you do that, you might find—like Harry—that your world turns upside down. That's a big risk to take.

Are you ready?

How Can I Live My Best Life Now?

At the beginning of the film *Moana*, everyone is happy on the island—except Moana. Even though she's the daughter of the chief, Moana doesn't quite belong. She longs for adventure. So she looks out to sea, and sings about how she's been "staring at the edge of the water" all her life.[1] Moana tries to forget adventure and fit in. But it doesn't work: the voice inside her sings a different song. "What is wrong with me?" she asks.

Perhaps you feel a bit the same: like you don't quite belong here. Perhaps when you read stories like the Harry Potter series—or see films like *Moana*—you find yourself staring at the edge of the water, wishing those magical worlds were real. That's how I felt when I first read *The Lord of the Rings*, and I didn't grow out of the feeling. In fact, I grew *into* it. The older I get, the more sure I am that the real world is *even more* magical than those imaginary ones. It's one of the reasons I believe in Jesus. The voice inside me sings a different song.

But following Jesus doesn't mean ignoring what I see around me. Just as Moana's dream of sailing out to sea doesn't mean abandoning her island but saving it, so, in this chapter, I want to suggest that following Jesus doesn't only give us a way to live our best life forever after we die. It also—in some unexpected ways—means living our best life together now.

Don't get me wrong. Jesus said that following him would be hard. Really hard. He said it would be like *dying* to yourself (Luke 9:23). But he also promised that following him was the way to *really* live: "I came that they may have life," he said, "and have it abundantly" (John 10:10).

Here are seven pieces of evidence to suggest Jesus was right.

Evidence #1: People Who Go to Church Are Happier and Healthier!

In 2007, a British guy called Christopher Hitchens wrote a bestselling book called, *God Is Not Great: How Religion Poisons Everything*. Lots of people believe that's true. They think we'd all be better off without religion. But since Hitchens wrote his book, a lot of evidence has come out to show that he was wrong! People who go to church at least once a week are happier, healthier, and longer lived than people who don't. Harvard professor Tyler VanderWeele is a world expert on this subject. He says that rather than religion being poisonous, going to church every week is like drinking a magical medicine.[2]

We all know that eating more fruits and vegetables is good for us. But it turns out that going to church once a week or more is equally good for you.[3] So if you really hate brussels sprouts but your parents make you eat them anyway, try asking if you can go to church instead! We all know smoking is bad for you. But going to church once a week or more is *almost* as good for you as stopping smoking![4] Professor VanderWeele's research has also found that children who are brought up going to church tend to end up being happier and having a greater sense of purpose in their lives than those raised non-religious.[5]

Going to church also helps us avoid things that are bad for us, like drinking too much alcohol or taking illegal drugs. This makes sense to me. A big reason people take drugs is that they want to feel something amazing that takes them out of their ordinary lives. But drugs make you feel good for a bit, and then they make you feel terrible—just like jumping off a building might feel really great while you were flying through the air, but terrible when you hit the ground. There are times when singing to Jesus with all sorts of other people at church makes me feel as if my heart will burst with joy! But instead of crashing to the ground afterward, I feel leftover happiness.

This is one of the reasons why people who go to church every week are less likely to get depressed. This doesn't mean Christians never suffer from depression. Many do. And sadly, some people (Christians and non-Christians) end up feeling so hopeless that they commit suicide. This is a terrible thing and many countries, schools, and cities have "suicide prevention" campaigns to make sure people who want to end their lives get help. But what you probably won't hear in suicide prevention education is that people who never go to church are as much as *five times more likely* to kill themselves than people who go every week.[6] In fact, Professor VanderWeele says that attending religious services weekly may be the best protection against suicide there is.

These benefits aren't just limited to Christianity. People who go to synagogue at least once a week also see positive effects in their health and happiness. But doing something non-religious, like going to a golf club once a week, and seeing the same people for a shared activity doesn't appear to have the same effect. It seems we humans thrive best when we worship in community together. We see this in the Bible, as believers meet together to sing and pray and read God's word (e.g., Acts 2:42; Colossians 3:16).

The benefits of going to church don't mean the Christian life isn't hard. It is. Jesus said that following him means picking up a cross, and people who carried crosses in Jesus's day were on the path to execution (Matthew 16:24). For some people across the world today, following Jesus *literally* means getting killed. On average, eleven Christians are executed for their faith *every day*. These people are trusting that life with Jesus forever is *better* than any life they can have here now. But even though it's hard and can be dangerous, following Jesus is also the best life we can live now. The apostle Paul (one of the first Christian leaders) was in prison and facing the possibility of execution for his faith when he wrote the letter to the Philippians. But instead of being sad about his circumstances, Paul kept telling the Philippians to rejoice (e.g., Philippians 1:18; 2:18; 3:1; 4:4).

In *Harry Potter and the Goblet of Fire*, Harry discovers he's going to need to swim underwater for a long time to complete one of his tasks, so he eats a special plant called "gillyweed" that makes him grow gills like a fish and webbed feet like a frog.[7] Harry's mission is still difficult and dangerous, but he's got what he needs to make it through. The Christian life is hard. But it's a life of joy and meaning and adventure, and the God who made us knows what helps us thrive. If we listen to both the Bible and researchers like Tyler VanderWeele, going to church weekly is a bit like taking gillyweed for life.

Evidence #2: Love Is the Most Important Thing

In the Disney film *Frozen*, Elsa's parents respond to her dangerous ice powers by cutting her off from her sister, Anna. But as Elsa grows up, her powers only get stronger. In the end, she stops trying to control them and in the famous song "Let It Go," she decides it's time to throw off all constraints. But by the end of the film, Elsa has realized that what she needed to control her powers wasn't unlimited freedom, it was love. And (as we'll see in chapter 7 of this book) despite what many songs and stories make us think, romantic love isn't the only kind that counts. As Elsa discovered, the love of friends and family is vital to our happiness.[8]

For seventy-five years, professors at Harvard have been running a study on well-being. Younger people in the study tended to expect that their happiness would depend on fame, wealth, and success. But they were wrong. Good relationships with family and friends were what kept people happiest and healthiest.[9]

For Christians, love is the heart of everything. The Bible says that "God is love" (1 John 4:8), and Jesus told his followers to "love one another as I have loved you" (John 15:12). So, according to the Bible, true love flows out of God's love. It doesn't just mean having "warm feelings" or "falling in love" with someone. It means being willing to sacrifice for others. In fact, the Bible says that we know what love *is* because Jesus laid down his life for us (1 John 3:16).

All of us want to be known and loved. The amazing message of the Bible is that the God who knows the very worst things about us also loved us enough to die in our place, so that—if we put our trust in him—we can live with him in happiness forever. People often like to say that love is the most powerful force in the universe. But Christians believe this is literally true.

Evidence #3: Helping Others Is Good for Us

Giving things up to help others feels hard. But Jesus made the strange claim that "it is more blessed to give than to receive" (Acts 20:35). He commanded, "Love your neighbor as yourself" (Mark 12:31), and despite being the rightful King of the whole world, he said he "came not to be served but to serve" and told his followers to live like that as well (Mark 10:44–45). Helping others can mean missing out ourselves. But Jesus made this stunning promise: "Whoever would save his life will lose it, but whoever loses his life for my sake will find it" (Matthew 16:25).

Jesus's promises are about eternal life. But following his commandments also has benefits now. The scientists and other experts who study the human mind and behavior have found that helping other people is actually good for us. For example, volunteering is good for our mental and physical health. Some studies have shown that caring for others is better for the carer than for the person being helped![10] This doesn't mean we'll never miss out by putting other people first. If you follow Jesus, the sacrifices will be real. But the truth is that God made us and knows how we work. In the end, selfishness makes us miserable.

We get a picture of this in the film *Aladdin*. When the evil Jafar finally gains control of the genie's lamp, he wishes for the genie to turn him into the most powerful being in the universe. This means becoming a genie himself. But Jafar forgets that genies must serve a master, and because Jafar is masterless, he gets trapped in the magical lamp. As this story illustrates, serving and worshiping ourselves makes us deeply unhappy in the end. It's not freedom; it's imprisonment.

Christians, like me, are often selfish. We don't live up to Jesus's standards. At heart, we're not good people: we're bad people who know we need Jesus's forgiveness every day. But there is good evidence that actively religious people are, on average, more generous than non-religious folk. For example, in America, people who go to church every week give three-and-a-half times as much money to charity and volunteer twice as much as people who never go to church.[11]

Evidence #4: Gratitude Is Good for Us

Growing up, I loved Christmas except for one thing. For every gift I received, my parents made me grind out a "thank you" card. (Now, any time I give a kid a gift, I tell their parents *not* to have them send me a card, because I remember how much I hated writing them myself!) But what if I hadn't hated writing those cards? What if I had focused on being *truly* thankful for the gift? Christmas would have probably been more fun for me. Psychologists have discovered that people who choose to be grateful (like for example, writing down the things they're thankful for every week) are happier and healthier than those who don't.[12]

If I'd listened to the Bible, I'd have known that already. Paul, who wrote a lot of the New Testament letters, went through all sorts of *terrible* things. He was beaten and shipwrecked and mocked and laughed at and finally killed for following Jesus. You might think he'd be a bit resentful! But instead he tells Christians to "rejoice always" and "give thanks in all circumstances" (1 Thessalonians 5:16, 18) because God is really in control. In fact, in Paul's letter to the church in Rome, he tells the Roman Christians that "all things work together for good" for those who love God (Romans 8:28). I cling to that promise when it feels like my life is going wrong. I try to remember that through all my ups and downs, through all my laughter and my tears, God is writing my storyline for good—like the most amazing author.

Christians have so many reasons to be thankful. We believe not only that God created all of us and gives us every good thing we have, but also that he offers us forgiveness and eternal life with him for free, so whatever happens to me here and now, the end of my story will be incredibly happy. As with the gifts I got at Christmas, someone else paid for me to have this gift. But this gift of relationship with God is more expensive than anything else I've ever been given. Jesus paid for it with his life when he died on the cross for me. So, for Christians, thankfulness isn't just like a positive-thinking technique you might learn at school. It's our joyful response to a life-making and life-saving God.

Evidence #5: Forgiveness Is Good for You!

Forgiving people can be hard. Jesus made it harder. One of his disciples suggested an upper limit of seven for how many times you should forgive someone. Jesus replied, "Not . . . seven times, but seventy-seven times" (Matthew 18:21–22). He taught his followers to pray, "Forgive us our sins, for we ourselves forgive everyone who is indebted to us" (Luke 11:4). And—amazingly—as he was hanging on the cross, Jesus prayed that God would forgive the soldiers who were executing him (Luke 23:34). Forgiven people, Jesus argued, must forgive.

Again, this turns out to be for our good. Experts have found that forgiveness is good for our minds and bodies.[13] This doesn't mean God doesn't care when we get hurt. (We'll talk more about this in chapter 9.) It also doesn't mean someone who has abused his or her power to hurt someone else should be allowed to keep that power. God is both loving and just, and the Bible teaches again and again that the vulnerable should be protected (e.g., Psalm 68:5). But God wants us to remember that final justice is in his hands, so we don't have to get back at people (Romans 12:19). Instead, Christians are called to forgive others as God has forgiven us.

Evidence #6: Grit Is Great!

The Lord of the Rings by J. R. R. Tolkien is one of my favorite books. Sam, one of the main characters, is a hobbit—like a human, but smaller and with extra hairy feet! Sam isn't rich or good-looking or particularly smart. He's just a gardener. But he really loves his friend Frodo, and he sticks with Frodo on their mission to destroy the evil ring. Frodo has been chosen to bear the ring. But Sam's passion and perseverance end up being vital to Frodo's success. Sam becomes a hero not because he is gifted and talented, but because he is loving and determined.

Do you ever wonder if you're smart enough or talented enough or good looking enough to succeed in life? I'm guessing we all wonder that sometimes. But it turns out that something psychologists call "grit" (which means being like Sam and sticking with a task we care about for a long time, even when it gets hard) makes more difference to our long-term success than intelligence or talent or good looks.[14]

We find the call to be gritty all over the Bible. Jesus said following him was like walking a hard road (Matthew 7:14). Peter (one of Jesus's first followers) calls Christians to have self-control and perseverance (2 Peter 1:6). The New Testament letter to the Hebrews urges Christians, "Let us run with endurance the race that is set before us, looking to Jesus, the founder and perfecter of our faith, who for the joy that was set before him endured the cross" (Hebrews 12:1–2). Rather than having us just struggle on alone though, Jesus promised to send his followers a Helper—the Spirit of God, who comes and lives with us if we accept Jesus as our Lord and Savior (John 14:16). God also gives us the companionship of other Christians along the way, just like Frodo had Sam. And when we fail, which we often will, we can rest knowing that Jesus has already won the victory.

Evidence #7: Love of Money Lets Us Down

When Aladdin rubs the lamp and the genie emerges to grant three wishes, he is shocked that Aladdin doesn't know what he wants. The genie says most people want money and power. But then he warns Aladdin:

> Do me a favor, do not drink from that cup. I promise you, there's not enough money and power on earth for you to be satisfied.[15]

We often think money will make us happy. In a 2016 survey of students, 82.3 percent checked becoming rich as an "essential" or "very important" life goal. But when people get some money, they tend to just want more. And more. And more. For people who are very poor, having a bit more money can help, but experts have discovered that choosing money over friends and family is a sure path to *unhappiness*.[16]

Once again, we find this wisdom already in the Bible. Paul calls the love of money "a root of all kinds of evils" (1 Timothy 6:10), and Jesus told a rich young man that he needed to give away all his money to the poor before he could follow Jesus. When that young man went away sad, Jesus said it was harder for a rich man to enter the kingdom of God than for a camel to go through the tiny hole where the thread goes in a needle (Matthew 19:16–26). Both in our lives today and in eternity, loving money lets us down. You can't buy happiness.

This doesn't mean we shouldn't work hard or earn money. Paul tells Christians that they should work to earn a living (2 Thessalonians 3:12) and to be able to support others in need (Ephesians 4:28). He encourages believers that whatever job they're doing, they should work at it with all their heart, as if working for the Lord (Colossians 3:23). Again, this turns out to be great advice. Experts have found that *how* we do a job matters more to our overall happiness than *what* the job is.[17]

You might want to do something that looks or sounds impressive when you grow up—like being a film star or a professional football player or a world-famous doctor or a best-selling author. It's not wrong to work hard toward getting a job like that. But being a gardener (like Sam) and working at it with all your heart as if you are working for the Lord might turn out to be better than being a film star or a football player. In fact, in Jesus's kingdom, the most seemingly unimportant people are actually the most important (Matthew 20:16).

What Do We Need?

So what does fill us up? It's easy to look at sports or film stars and wish we had their lives. But when superstars like singer Taylor Swift or Olympic athlete Michael Phelps open up about their lives, we often discover that fame and success have left them feeling empty and depressed. Famous people have a spotlight on them all the time. Their success becomes their identity, and their fans start to worship them. But we humans aren't designed for that. Like planets orbiting the sun, we're meant to orbit around God. We're not meant to be the center of our own little universe. Atheist psychologist Jonathan Haidt summarizes our psychological needs like this: "Just as plants need sun, water, and good soil to thrive, people need love, work, and a connection to something larger."[18] Following Jesus gives us all these things.

Daniel Hastings is a world expert in space science and a professor of aeronautics and astronautics at MIT. He became a Christian when he was a teenager in England, after a search for meaning and purpose in his life. "I have found Jesus Christ to provide the purpose and meaning for which I was searching," Professor Hastings recalls. "He has led and guided me ever since."[19]

Staring at the edge of the water, Moana wondered if there were any adventures before her and asked how far she'd go. So far in my life, I've found that following Jesus is the surest path to love, joy, and adventure. I still feel as if I don't belong at times. But that's something Jesus followers should expect. Like Harry Potter growing up in the Muggle world, we also don't really belong here. We belong to Jesus's much more magical world, and that world's just starting to break in.

- Experts have found that going to church is really good for your mental and physical health. People who go to church weekly tend to be:
  - happier
  - healthier
  - longer-lived
  - less likely to suffer from depression
  - less likely to commit suicide
  - less likely to take drugs or abuse alcohol
  - more likely to volunteer
  - more generous with their money

- Psychologists have also found that many of the things that the Bible teaches are good for us, including:
  - going to church
  - putting loving relationships first
  - helping others
  - being thankful
  - forgiving others
  - sticking with hard tasks in the long term
  - not loving money

- Jesus never promised us an easy life now. In fact, he said the opposite. But following Jesus and living as the Bible calls us to live turns out to be really good for us—even here and now.

Isn't Christianity against Diversity?

Three years ago, I was sitting on a plane next to a twelve-year-old boy from Ghana in West Africa. He was wearing three wristbands. The first one said, "unaccompanied minor," because he was flying alone. The second said, "Commitment to kindness." The third said, "Walking with Jesus." This young man had only recently moved to America. I asked him if it felt different being a Christian in Ghana versus in America. He said "Yes, because there are *lots* of Christians in Africa, but there aren't so many in America." I asked him why he thought that was, and he said, "Because Americans believe in diversity."

The word *diversity* is everywhere today. Its basic meaning is "differentness." But we often use it to mean accepting and welcoming people who are different from us. There are three main reasons why people think that Christianity is *against* diversity. First, people think that Christianity is basically a white, Western religion. They see the ways in which white Westerners (like me) have at times harmed and oppressed people from other racial and cultural backgrounds, rather than accepting and welcoming them, so they think Christianity is a way for white Westerners to keep their power over others. That's the concern we'll focus on in this chapter. Second, Christians believe that Jesus is the *only* way to God, and people think this is disrespectful and unloving toward those who believe in other religions. We'll explore this concern in chapter 3. Third, people think Christians are hateful and intolerant toward those who are different in other ways: for example, people who identify as gay or transgender. We'll talk about that in chapters 7 and 8.

People tend to lump all different kinds of diversity together. But throughout this book, we'll see that there are different *kinds* of difference: some related to the way we were born, others to the feelings we have, the choices we make, or the things we believe. We need to understand different kinds of difference differently! But across all kinds of difference, we'll see one basic, overarching theme: Jesus commands not just tolerance of those who are different from us, but deep, expensive, unrelenting *love*.

Jesus Created Diversity

One of my favorite parts of the Bible is the beginning of John's Gospel. It goes like this:

> In the beginning was the Word, and the Word was with God, and the Word was God. He was in the beginning with God. All things were made through him, and without him was not any thing made that was made. In him was life, and the life

was the light of men. The light shines in the darkness, and the darkness has not overcome it. (John 1:1–5)

As the story goes on, we discover that this "Word" is Jesus. If what John says is true, it means that Jesus *invented* diversity. He made people from Europe and Africa and Asia and South America. He made you, and he made me, and he made the Ghanaian boy sitting next to me on my flight. He made black Americans and white Americans and Native Americans and Asian Americans. He made people whose parents have similar racial heritage (like me), and people whose parents have different racial heritage—like my beautiful friend Catherine, whose mother came from Ghana and whose father came from Korea. Jesus himself was a brown-skinned, Middle Eastern, Jewish man. But he delights to make people with all different kinds of skin color and eye color and hair type and body type. Jesus loves to be creative, so he makes people beautifully different. It's helpful for all of us to remember this when we feel bad about how we look.

When I first met my mother-in-law, she showed me photos of my husband when he was a baby. Between you and me, he looked pretty terrible. He had about fifteen chins and lots of funny features. But when I laughed at how he looked, his mother was not happy with me. That was her baby I was laughing at, and in her eyes, he was *extremely* cute! When God looks at you—however imperfect you might think you are or however different from others you feel—he sees his beautiful child, and he delights in you. What's more, despite our physical differences, the very first book of the Bible tells us an amazing thing: God made all humans *in his image* and *after his likeness* (Genesis 1:26–27).

What does this mean?

We're All Made in God's Image

As I write this, my son is one year old. People often tell me he looks just like my husband—except that he's a baby with fat, smooth cheeks, and my husband is a grown man with a scruffy beard! The idea of a child looking like a parent is part of what the Bible means by us being made in God's image. But there are two reasons we know this is *not* about how we look physically. First, until God became man in the person of Jesus, God did not have a physical body that we *could* look like! Second, because God made so many different people *all equally* in his image, we can't say that God looks like one kind of person. My son might be the baby-faced image of his dad. But every human infant in the world—whatever his or her racial heritage—is made in the image of God.

We learn more about what being in God's image means when Jesus says that anyone who has seen him has seen the Father (John 14:9) and when Paul calls Jesus the "the image of the invisible God" (Colossians 1:15). We know almost nothing about what Jesus looked like physically. We can guess from where Jesus came from and the culture he lived in that he had brown skin and a beard. (People have often painted pictures of Jesus with pale skin, like mine, but that's not accurate.) We also have a little hint from a prophecy in the book of Isaiah that Jesus wasn't especially good-looking (Isaiah 53:2). But while we don't know much about Jesus's body, we know a *lot* about his character: how he lived, how he thought, and what he said and did. All these things give us glimpses of what God is like and how we too might image him.

None of us image God perfectly—as Jesus did—because he is holy and we are all messed up with sin. But we are *all* made in

God's image. It doesn't matter how young or old we are, if we do really well in school or if we have a learning disability, if we are able bodied or unable to walk or talk or see, if we're male or female, if we're black or white or Asian or Hispanic or Native American or a beautiful mix of different racial backgrounds. We're all made in God's image. So Jesus invented *diversity*, by creating people with all sorts of different bodies and minds, but he also invented *equality*, because we are all equally made in God's image. When people look down on others because of their racial background or body type or mental ability, they're going against God's plan and they're not listening to what the Bible says.

Jesus Commanded Love across Difference

People often think that the Bible was written by white, Western people. But it wasn't. The Bible was written by brown-skinned Jewish people from the Middle East, and it teaches us to love those who are different from us. Jesus said God's most important commandments were first "love the Lord your God with all your heart and with all your soul and with all your mind and with all your strength" and second "love your neighbor as yourself" (Mark 12:29–31). When someone asked Jesus, "Who is my neighbor?" he told a story called the parable of the good Samaritan, in which a man from a hated racial and cultural group showed love to someone who was different from him. So Jesus puts love across differences right at the center of his moral teaching.

In his own life, Jesus repeatedly broke through racial and cultural boundaries. For example, he made friends with a Samaritan woman at a well, despite the fact that Jews in his day hated Samaritans (John 4:4–26). And after Jesus's death and resurrection, he told his disciples to "Go therefore and make disciples of all nations!" (Matthew 28:19).

In the book of Acts (which tells us the story of the first Christians) we see Jesus's followers preaching the good news about Jesus to people from all sorts of countries—from Iran, Iraq, and Turkey in the Middle East to Egypt and Libya in Africa (Acts 2:9–11). In Acts 8, we meet the first known black Christian: an Ethiopian man (Acts 8:26–40). And in the New Testament letters, we see how Jesus brought people from all different racial and cultural backgrounds together. For example, Paul wrote to Christians living in Turkey:

> Here there is not Greek and Jew, circumcised and uncircumcised, barbarian, Scythian, slave, free; but Christ is all, and in all. (Colossians 3:11)

This might not make much sense to us. (For instance, I had to look up who the Scythians were: it turns out they were nomadic warriors who lived in Siberia and liked tattoos!) But Paul is calling out some of the major racial, social, and national differences of his time and place. In America today, he might say, "Here there is neither European American nor African American, neither Asian American nor Latina/Latino American, neither rich nor poor, neither Californian nor Texan, but Christ is all, and in all." Jesus calls people from all different backgrounds to be his "body" on earth together (1 Corinthians 12:27).

If we look back through history, we'll see that Jesus's teaching was the original foundation on which people built the idea that all humans are equally valuable and that you should love people from different countries and races and backgrounds. People in the

Roman Empire didn't think that at all. In fact, most belief systems throughout history have *not* taught that all humans are equally valuable. I recently finished reading a book called *Dominion: How the Christian Revolution Remade the World* by British historian Tom Holland. He is not a Christian himself, but he shows from history that it's really because of Christianity that people today (whether they identify as Christians or not) think that all humans should be valued equally, regardless of their race or sex or nationality, and that you should love people who are different from you. Jesus really did invent diversity! But we also see many examples in history of Christians hating, hurting, and enslaving people of other racial backgrounds, despite what the Bible clearly teaches. So what are we to make of this?

"Them" and "Us"

A few months ago, I saw a video of a little white boy and a little black boy running down the street to hug each other. It was a lovely image, and people were saying this video showed that we humans naturally love people who are different from us. There is some truth in this. Last week, I was talking with my eight-year-old daughter about some horrible examples of violence toward black people. She is white, but her three best friends in her class at school are all black, and she simply cannot understand why people would treat others differently just because of their skin color. But most people in the world *haven't* had the chance to grow up really knowing people of different racial backgrounds, and we humans naturally form groups of "them" and "us."

For much of our history, humans have lived in tribes and fought against people from other tribes. Today, most humans don't live in tribes in quite the same way. But nonetheless, we find ways to make "in-groups" and "out-groups": people we want to hang out with and people we don't. We might divide people according to whether they like the right music, or wear the right clothes, or whether they're rich or smart or funny or seen as especially good looking. We all want to be in the in-group and fear being in the out-group. You see this in middle school and high school. But people don't grow out of it. Adults are desperate to belong as well. And one way that people have often split up into groups is by their racial or cultural background—especially if one racial group has more power than the other.

We see terrible examples of this in American history. For instance, for hundreds of years, black people were kept as slaves by white people. They were made to work hard for no money and were often beaten and ill treated. Even before they got to America, millions of enslaved Africans died on the ships that were transporting them. My own country (Britain) transported over three million Africans on slave ships during this time. After slavery was made illegal in the US, black Americans were not given the same rights as white Americans. They weren't allowed to live in the same neighborhoods, go to the same schools, use the same bathrooms, or ride in the same sections of buses. Even after they got the same legal rights, black Americans have continued to face prejudice, discrimination, and violence. People made in God's own image—people for whom Jesus came to die—have been treated like their lives just didn't matter. This is an offense against God.

Throughout this history, many of the leaders who have fought against this kind of injustice have been Christians: for example, William Wilberforce led the campaign to abolish slavery in Britain;

Harriet Tubman escaped from slavery and risked her life to help other enslaved people break free; the Reverend Dr. Martin Luther King Jr. led the civil rights movement in the 1960s; and lawyer Bryan Stevenson founded the Equal Justice Initiative in Alabama in 1989 and wrote the best-selling book *Just Mercy*. These leaders (and many others) were driven by their Christian faith. But sadly, many of the people who owned slaves in the first place, many of the people who opposed the civil rights movement, and many who have engaged in racism since have identified as Christians too.

So does this mean that if you care about racial justice you should *not* be a Christian? No. First, as we have seen, the Bible is the *basis* for love across racial difference. But there's another reason too.

The Miracle of the Black Church

You might think that the history of black people being enslaved and abused by white people who claimed to be Christians would mean that black people in America were the *least* likely to be Christians themselves. But the opposite is true. Amazingly, many enslaved Africans became followers of Jesus. They saw that Jesus was on the side of the oppressed, not the oppressors. They saw that Jesus cared about their suffering and that their lives mattered to him so much that he was willing to die for them. They read in the Old Testament that God's people had once themselves been enslaved in Egypt and that God had rescued them from slavery, so they put their hope in God to save them too.

The 2019 film *Harriet* tells the story of Harriet Tubman, who escaped slavery herself and went on to help hundreds of others escape. She was nicknamed "Moses" after the man who led God's people out of slavery in the biblical book of Exodus. Like Moses, she was trusting God to guide her as she did the dangerous work of helping people escape slavery. And like many of the leading black abolitionists, Harriet Tubman saw her faith in Jesus as the most important thing in her life.

When Frederick Douglass (another leading anti-slavery campaigner) became a Christian at age thirteen, he remembered how God changed his heart like this:

> I loved all mankind, slaveholders not excepted, though I abhorred slavery more than ever. I saw the world in a new light, and my great concern was to have everybody converted.[1]

Likewise, when a woman named Sojourner Truth traveled around speaking against the slavery that she herself had previously endured, she said she always had one text: "When I found Jesus."[2]

People becoming Christians even while they were enslaved to other people who called themselves Christians was the beginning of the black church in America. The black church was the driving force of the civil rights movement led by Baptist pastor Martin Luther King Jr. Today, black Americans are almost 10 percent more likely to identify as Christians than white Americans, and nearly half of all black Americans go to church every week, versus only a third of white Americans.[3] Black women in America are particularly likely to be Christians, while white men are more likely than others to be atheists.[4]

So what about in the rest of the world?

Jesus Delivers Diversity

Today, Christianity is the most diverse belief system in the world, with roughly equal numbers of Christians living in Europe, Latin

America, and Africa, and with a rapidly growing church in Asia.[5] Christianity isn't just for people from one country, one culture, one race, or one language. It's for people from every country, every culture, every race, and every language! In the book of Revelation (the last book in the Bible) we get a glimpse of how things are going to be at the end of time, when a "great multitude that no one could number, from every nation, from all tribes and peoples and languages" will worship Jesus together (Revelation 7:9). If you're a Christian, this is your destiny! And even now, it's becoming a reality.

The church community group that meets at our house every week includes black people, white people, and Asian people. We have members who immigrated to America from Ghana, Ethiopia, Singapore, England, and Romania. We have people who grew up in Christian families, and people who only just became believers in Jesus last year. We grew up speaking many different languages and we come from many different places, but we are one body together because we all trust in Jesus and our group is a little picture of the global church. Despite all the sins of racism committed by Christians over the centuries, Christianity is the greatest movement for diversity in all of history.

The Ghanaian boy I sat next to on the plane thought there were fewer Christians in America because Americans believe in diversity. But he and I are evidence of the diversity at the heart of Christianity. He's male, I'm female. He grew up in Ghana, I grew up in England. He's black, I'm white. He's a kid, I'm an adult. But because we're both "walking with Jesus," we belong together, not just now, but for all eternity.

- God created all human beings of every race and ethnicity equally in his image.
- Jesus was a brown-skinned, Jewish man from the Middle East, who commanded his followers to love those who are different from them and to make disciples of all nations.
- Jesus's life and teachings are the original reason we believe in human equality, and they are still the best foundation for racial diversity.
- Christians have often failed to obey Jesus's commandments and instead have hated, abused, and enslaved people who have a different racial background: for example, millions of Africans were transported as slaves to America.
- Despite this evil, many enslaved Africans became Christians themselves, and their descendants today are the most likely Americans to be followers of Jesus.
- Many leaders who have fought against racial injustice have been driven by their faith in Jesus.
- Jesus calls people from every tribe and language and nation to follow him.
- Today, Christianity is the most diverse belief system in the world, with roughly equal numbers of Christians living in Europe, Latin America, and Africa, and a rapidly growing church in Asia.
- Christianity isn't against racial and cultural diversity. It's the most racially and culturally diverse movement in all of history.

Can Jesus Be True for You but Not for Me?

On February 23, 2019, a Nigerian Christian named Oluwole Ilesanmi stood outside a train station in London preaching to people as they walked by. Two British police officers came up to him and gave him a choice: go away or be arrested.

"I will not go away," Mr. Ilesanmi replied. "I need to tell them the truth, because Jesus is the only way, the truth, and the life!"

"Nobody wants to listen to that," said one of the officers. "They want you to go away."

"You don't want to listen to that?" Mr. Ilesanmi replied. "You will listen when you're dead. You will listen when you are dead!" So he was arrested.

In Western countries like Britain and America, most people think it's okay to say you're a Christian, so long as you leave other people alone. I can say that Jesus is true for me. But if, like Mr. Ilesanmi, I say that Jesus is the way, the truth, and the life for everyone everywhere (John 14:6)—regardless of their culture, race, or current religious beliefs—that's seen as offensive.

So what are we to make of this? Can Jesus be true for me, but not for you?

The Elephant in the Room

A few months ago, I saw a car bumper sticker that read, "My God is too big for any one religion." When people put stickers like that on their cars, their message is that it's okay to believe in God, but that it's arrogant and ignorant to say that one religion is true and that others are not. Sometimes people tell a story about an elephant to explain this view.

In the story, an elephant walked into a village where everyone was blind. The villagers were fascinated by the strange creature. One villager touched the elephant's leg and said the elephant was like a tree. Another touched its ear and said the elephant was like a fan. A third touched its trunk and said the elephant was like a snake, and so on. Soon arguments began to break out. All the villagers had felt different parts of the elephant and discovered a piece of the truth about this amazing animal. But because they were blind, they couldn't see the whole elephant, so they didn't see how all these different truths could fit together. In the same way, people claim that different religions hold pieces of the truth about God, but no one religion holds it all. For this reason, people say we shouldn't argue about which religion is right. We should just learn from each religion, because between all of us, we might just get the whole truth about God. But there are several problems with the elephant story and with the argument it represents.

First, the villagers are blind, but the person telling the story can see. It might sound respectful to Christians, Muslims, Buddhists, Hindus, and Jews to say that if they saw the big picture, they'd all realize they each held a piece of the truth. But it's actually not respectful at all. If you say this, what you're *really* saying is that Christians, Muslims, Buddhists, Hindus, and Jews are all blind and you alone can see!

Second, the elephant story has no place or explanation for people who change their religious beliefs, like my friend Praveen Sethupathy, who grew up Hindu, but started following Jesus when he was a student at Cornell University (where he is now a professor).[1] Or my friend Mark Shepard, who was raised Jewish, became an atheist as a teenager, and then started following Jesus when he was a student at Harvard University (where he is now a professor).[2] Both Praveen and Mark would now say that the religions they were raised with were wrong on some extremely important points and that Jesus is the way, the truth, and the life.

This doesn't mean that Christians believe all other religions are wrong on every point. Because Christianity springs out of Judaism and Jews and Christians share the Old Testament scriptures, Mark is able to agree with many of the Jewish beliefs he was raised with, while also believing that Jesus is the only way to God. Hinduism has far less in common with Christianity, so Praveen would now say that many Hindu beliefs about God are wrong. But this doesn't mean Praveen has stopped loving the Indian culture with which he was raised. He loves the culture he comes from and wants to pass as much of that cultural heritage on to his kids as possible.

As we saw in chapter 2, people from all different cultures can be followers of Jesus. Christians can eat different food, wear different clothes, speak different languages, and enjoy different music depending on their cultural background. But like Praveen, Mark, and Oluwole Ilesanmi, Christians from all different cultures believe that Jesus is the way, the truth, and the life, and that no one can come to God except through him (John 14:6).

The third problem with the idea that all religions are equally true is that different religions contradict each other—not just in small ways that don't matter too much, but in really big ways. Here's one important example.

At the center of the Christian faith is the claim that Jesus Christ died on a cross and was physically raised from the dead three days later. If this is not true, then Christianity is not true. As Paul puts it, "If Christ has not been raised, your faith is futile and you are still in your sins" (1 Corinthians 15:17). In other words, without the resurrection, Christianity is useless. But if we look at the two other major religions that have *most* in common with Christianity—Judaism and Islam—we find that Jews and Muslims disagree with this central claim of Christianity. Jews believe that Jesus died and stayed dead. Muslims believe that Jesus didn't die but just appeared to die, and that he was taken up to heaven. Christians believe that Jesus died and rose to life again (see, for example, 1 Corinthians 15:3–4).

As a Christian, I believe that Jesus was physically raised from the dead. I think there is good evidence to support that belief, though we can't prove it beyond reasonable doubt. But there's one thing we can all know for sure: Jesus was either physically raised from the dead or he wasn't. If we took a video camera back two thousand years and set it up outside his tomb, we'd either see him coming out or not. What we *can't* say is that Christians, Muslims, and Jews are *all* right about Jesus. He is either the resurrected King of the universe, who defeated sin and death, or he is not. Jesus's claims about himself are outrageous. But they sounded just as outrageous in the first century as they do now.

The Puzzle Piece That Doesn't Fit

At the time when Jesus walked this earth, there were even more religions than there are today. In the world today, three out of four people say they belong to one of four religions: Christianity (31 percent), Islam (24 percent), Hinduism (15 percent), or Buddhism (7 percent). But at the time when Jesus was born, people believed in all sorts of gods and goddesses. Very few people were monotheists (people who believe there is only one God). Most people were polytheists (people who believe there are lots of gods). If you've read the Percy Jackson series, you'll know about some of the gods and goddesses the Greeks and Romans believed in. So, if Jesus's followers had said he was another god, they'd have fit right in. Jesus would have just been one more piece in a great big god-and-goddess puzzle! But his disciples didn't say that, because they couldn't. Jesus didn't claim to be *a* god. He claimed to be *the one*, true God in the flesh. He was like the puzzle piece that just won't fit, no matter how hard you try to bend the edges.

Most people today don't believe there are *many* gods. But lots of people in our society believe that there are many ways to God and that God can mean different things to different people. They say Jesus can be true for me but not for you. Some people even say that Jesus *didn't* claim to be God, but that he was just a good teacher like other religious leaders. But Jesus shocked the people of his day because he *was* claiming to be God.

The Jewish people of Jesus's day knew that only God could forgive sins (Mark 2:7). But Jesus claimed *he* could forgive sins (Mark 2:5, 10). Some Jews at the time believed that God would raise his faithful followers from the dead at the end of time. But Jesus said, "I *am* the resurrection and the life" (John 11:25). Jewish people believed that God had authority over heaven and earth. But Jesus claimed that all authority in heaven and on earth had been given to him (Matthew 28:18). Therefore from his own words, Jesus cannot be just a good teacher, or one option among many gods or ways, because he claims that he is "*the* way, and *the* truth, and *the* life" (John 14:6) and that if we have seen him, we have seen God (John 14:9). This is what Mr. Ilesanmi was telling the London commuters. But why did he need to tell them? Why couldn't he just mind his own business, like the officers wanted?

The Ship Is Going Down

The famous film *Titanic* adds a fictional love story about two young people, Jack and Rose, to a true story about a massive boat called the *Titanic*. Everyone believed the boat was so big and strong and modern that it couldn't sink. In 1912, thousands of people boarded the *Titanic* in England to sail to America. But in the middle of the ocean, it ran into an iceberg and sank.

In the film, Rose is staying in the expensive, first-class part of the boat, and Jack is staying in the cheap, third-class part. But they manage to meet and fall in love. While they are out on deck together, they see the iceberg just as the ship crashes into it. A little later, Rose has a conversation with the man who built the ship:

Rose: Mr. Andrews! I saw the iceberg, and I see it in your eyes . . . please, tell me the truth!

Thomas Andrews: The ship will sink.

Rose: Are you certain?

Thomas Andrews: Yes, in an hour or so, all of this will be at the bottom of the Atlantic.[3]

At this point in the film, most people on the ship don't know the ship is going down. They are just carrying on enjoying themselves. The orchestra is playing. Food and drinks are being served. But Rose knows. She also knows from Mr. Andrews that there aren't enough lifeboats for everyone on the ship to be saved. He says to her,

> Please tell only who you must, I don't want to be responsible for a panic. And get to a boat quickly. Don't wait. You remember what I told you about the boats?[4]

When I was a teenager, I heard a man named Rico Tice explain that if the message of Jesus is true, it's like we're all sailing on the *Titanic*. Jesus warns us that without his offer of salvation, everyone is facing God's judgment as surely as the people on that ship were facing drowning if they didn't get to a lifeboat. The people on the ship are like the London commuters who ignored Mr. Ilesanmi. They're just going about their daily lives and don't think they have a problem. Christians are in a similar situation to Rose at this point in the film. She knows everyone is in deadly danger. If she tells people, they'll have a chance to get to a lifeboat. But Jesus isn't like Mr. Andrews. Jesus doesn't say, "Tell only who you must!" He says, "Tell everyone!"(Matthew 28:18–20). He doesn't say, "There aren't enough lifeboats to save all these people." He says, "Whoever believes in me, though he die, yet shall he live" (John 11:25). Jesus is the lifeboat. He's got room for anyone who jumps. It's not offensive and unloving for Christians to tell people that the ship is going down and to plead with them to run to Jesus. It's offensive and unloving *not* to!

We Should Respect People ... and Try to Persuade Them

If you're a follower of Jesus, what does this mean? Should we stand in the streets like Mr. Ilesanmi and tell people that Jesus is the way, the truth, and the life? Should we walk around the corridors at school and tell everyone we meet that they must run to the lifeboat of Jesus because the ship is going down? What guidance does the Bible give us?

Jesus told his followers to go and make disciples of all nations (Matthew 28:19). Just as fish need to swim, Christians need to share their faith. Sometimes, this means standing in the street like Mr. Ilesanmi. But often people will be more willing to listen to us about Jesus if they know and trust us.

Imagine if Rose had wanted everyone on the *Titanic* to believe the ship was sinking. She could have run around the ship shouting. Lots of people would have heard the message. But they might just have thought she was crazy and ignored her. If she wanted strangers to believe her, she might have been better off introducing herself, getting to know them a bit, talking to them calmly, and explaining what she'd seen and been told by Mr. Andrews. Then, she could tell them to tell their family and friends. In a similar way, it is often better for Christians to get to know other people, listen to their stories, find out what they believe and why, and love them as neighbors, while also telling them about Jesus. People tend to listen most to someone they trust.

The Bible also gives us guidance about how we should talk to people who aren't yet followers of Jesus. Peter was one of Jesus's most enthusiastic disciples. He said that Christians should always be ready to give a reason for their faith in Jesus, but that they should do this with "gentleness and respect" (1 Peter 3:15). Paul—who hated Christians and went around arresting them before he met Jesus himself (see Acts 9)—said we should try to persuade others to put their trust in Jesus, but that we should do this only driven by Jesus's love (2 Corinthians 5:11–14). If we're followers of Jesus, we must not give people the idea that we're saying we are better than they are. Paul said Jesus came to save sinners, and Paul called himself the *worst* (1 Timothy 1:15). Being a Christian means admitting you're a helpless sinner, not thinking you're better than other people. But if the ship is going down, it's not arrogant to tell people the truth and point them to the lifeboat. It's deeply unloving not to.

According to British law, Mr. Ilesanmi should not have been arrested, and he was released soon afterward. But in many other countries today, people are being arrested and even executed for saying that Jesus is the only way. They're risking their lives so that others have a chance to believe in Jesus and find eternal life in him. I sometimes find it hard to talk about my faith in Jesus, because I think people will be offended, or say that I'm arrogant or ignorant, or not want to be friends with me anymore. But if I really love my friends, I need to tell them the truth. And Jesus is the only way, the truth, and the life.

- Saying all religions are equal paths to God sounds respectful, but it actually isn't, because it doesn't take the truth claims of any religion seriously.
- The major world religions disagree on really important questions: for example, whether Jesus rose from the dead or not.
- Either Jesus was raised or he was not. This is a question of history, not just perspective or opinion. All religions can't be right.
- Jesus didn't just claim he was *a* god, he claimed he was *the one and only* God in the flesh, with power over heaven and earth and the right to forgive sins.
- If Jesus is the only way to God, and if he has given Christians the job of telling others about him, then it's disrespectful and unloving toward others not to pass on the message.
- When Christians share the message of Jesus with others, they must do so with gentleness and respect and be motivated by love.
- Being a Christian doesn't mean thinking you're a good person. It means believing you're a helpless sinner and your only hope is Jesus.

Can't We Just Be Good without God?

I n a comic scene in the film *Wreck-It-Ralph,* Ralph attends a support group for bad characters. Ralph is a gentle giant, who plays the villain in the "Fix-It Felix" video game. For years, the villains from the other arcade games have been inviting Ralph to join their group. But Ralph hasn't joined. Unlike them, he doesn't *want* to be a bad guy. He wants to be good. But he's stuck with the bad-guy role in his game. At the end of the support group meeting, the villains stand up, join hands, and chant "the bad guy affirmation":

> I'm bad, and that's good.
> I will never be good, and that's not bad.
> There's no one I'd rather be than me.[1]

The chant is funny because it's ridiculous! But it also raises some important questions: What *is* the difference between good and evil? Who gets to decide? Is there even such a thing as good and evil, or do we all just get to decide for ourselves?

Wait a minute! You might say. *Surely everyone knows the difference between good and evil. Whether we are Christian or Muslim or Hindu or atheist, we can all agree on the basics. Good is treating everyone as equal, caring for the people who are suffering, loving people who are different from us, and not hurting anyone. Bad is like racism, bullying, starting wars, and killing babies. Easy!*

We think all this is obvious. But if we rewind time to when Jesus was born, we find that it's not so simple.

Back to Ancient Rome

When Jesus was born, there were no movie theaters. Instead, there were *amphitheaters*—massive, open-air buildings, like football stadiums, where thousands of people went to watch shows. Some of the most popular shows involved gladiators fighting each other. The audience loved watching, just like people love watching football games or action movies today. But in the gladiatorial contest, people *actually* died.

Imagine how you'd feel if you went to a football game and someone *actually* died? Officials would stop the game at once. You might never want to see a football game again. But in Jesus's time, people went to shows like this because they *wanted* to see people die. They thought it was fun. The people who died were usually slaves or prisoners of war, so no one cared enough about them to feel sad. At that time, people didn't think that all human lives were precious. People cared about their families and friends and those like them. But slaves or prisoners or people of other nationalities weren't *their* people, so they could enjoy watching them die, like you might enjoy watching a battle in an action film.

At that time too, people generally agreed that men were more important than women, that slavery was just fine, and that children and babies were property rather than precious people. If you had a baby you didn't want—especially if the baby was a girl or had a disability—it was okay just to leave the baby outside somewhere to die. No one would think you were a bad person for doing that. Someone else might find the baby and bring her up as a slave, or else the baby would just die. There were no laws against such practices. Babies were property, so you could throw them out if you liked.

It wasn't that people at that time didn't care about good and evil. The ancient Romans had moral rules. For example, they valued honor, bravery in battle, and loyalty to Rome. But their rules were different from ours because their beliefs were different. If you look at the history of how we came to believe that it's not okay to enjoy watching innocent people getting killed, or that men and women are equally valuable, or that poor people should be cared for, or that it's not okay to leave a baby outside to die, the answer is one person: Jesus.

Jesus Made All Lives Count

When parents brought babies and little kids to Jesus, his disciples told them to go away. They thought Jesus was too important to bother with babies. But Jesus told his disciples off. He took the babies in his arms and blessed them. In fact, he said that if anyone didn't have faith like a little child, they couldn't enter God's kingdom (Matthew 19:13–15; Mark 10:13–16; Luke 18:15–17). Babies and children mattered to Jesus.

In Jesus's day, people who had a disease called leprosy were forced to live away from everyone else because it was a terrible sickness and was thought to be highly contagious. You'd never touch someone with leprosy, because you might get sick yourself. But Jesus touched people with leprosy and healed them (Matthew 8:1–4). Sick people and outcasts mattered to Jesus.

Jesus was Jewish, and Jewish people in Jesus's day hated Samaritans. But Jesus shocked his hearers by telling a story where a Samaritan was the moral hero (Luke 10:25–37), and Jesus made friends with a Samaritan woman, who ended up telling all her Samaritan friends about him (John 4:1–42). People of different races and cultures mattered to Jesus.

Time and again, Jesus looked out for the people no one else bothered with: sick people, poor people, people of different races, women, children, people others thought were too sinful to be loved by God. He cared for them and welcomed them. And he taught his followers to do the same. This is why Christians were the first people to invent hospitals, where poor people who got sick could be cared for. This is why Christians started picking up the babies other people had abandoned and taking care of them. This is why Christians started looking after not only other Christians who were poor, but also poor people who were not Christians. The fourth century Roman emperor Julian wrote a letter complaining about this, because it was making the people who followed the Roman gods look bad! But the gods in Roman religious stories didn't care about the poor, so it wasn't surprising if their followers didn't either.

Even today, the reason we think it's wrong to kill babies or hate people from other racial backgrounds or fail to take care of sick people and poor people is not because it's obvious. It's because of Jesus. Our ideas of good and bad have been deeply shaped by his teaching. And if we cut Jesus out of the picture, we stop having proper reasons to believe these things.

In chapter 2, I mentioned a book called *Dominion: How the Christian Revolution Remade the World* by British historian Tom Holland, who shows from history that our beliefs about right and wrong and the equal value of all humans came to us from Christianity. But Holland is not the only non-Christian historian to make this point. In 2014, a historian called Yuval Noah Harari published a best selling book called *Sapiens: A Brief History of Humankind*. In it, he says that the idea that human beings are equally morally valuable and that there are such things as "human rights"—basic protections that every human being is entitled to—is just a fiction made up by Christianity.[2] Speaking as someone who doesn't believe in God, Harari says human beings have "no natural rights, just as spiders, hyenas, and chimpanzees have no natural rights."[3]

If Christianity isn't true and there isn't a God who made us in his image and told us to love our neighbors as ourselves, then Harari is correct: we have no basis for believing that all humans are equally precious and that we should protect their human rights. We have no basis for saying racism is wrong. We have no basis for saying babies shouldn't be left outside to die. If there is no God, these things are just our preferences and opinions. They're not universal truths to which everyone must agree.

You may have watched cartoons when you were younger, where a character runs off a cliff so fast that he keeps on running even though there isn't any ground beneath his feet. Then, suddenly, he realizes the ground is gone. You see the look of panic on his face and then he falls. That's a bit like what we're doing if we still believe in human rights without believing in Jesus. The ground has gone from underneath our feet.

Are Unborn Babies Human Beings?

One area where we can see the Christian belief that all humans are equally valuable eroding is in our beliefs about babies. As we have seen, Jesus changed the way babies were valued. Rather than being possessions that could be thrown out if they weren't wanted, Jesus made babies seem precious. Because every human is made in the image of God, Christians believe that unborn babies—even at the beginning of their development—are incredibly valuable. But many people today think women should have the right to end the life of their unborn babies (also known as having an abortion) if they choose. They would say they are "pro-choice" and argue that pregnancy, childbirth, and raising kids is hard and disruptive to women's lives and that women should have the right to choose what they do with their own bodies.

In general, of course, we should all agree that women have the right to make choices about their own bodies. It is also true that women sometimes find themselves in desperate circumstances where having a baby would be especially hard. Women in these situations need care, support, and help—and sadly many women who have abortions do so because they don't think they will get the help they need. But we would also all agree that there should be limits to our freedom when our choices affect other people. For example, I don't have the right to choose to punch you in the face. I would be choosing to do something with my own body, but it would be something that harmed your body. What's more, if you were stuck dangling over the edge of a cliff and I was on the top of the cliff holding your hand, I wouldn't have the right to choose to let go—even if holding onto your hand was really hurting my arm. I'd have to hold onto your hand for as long as possible to keep you alive until more help came.

The question at the heart of the abortion debate is whether an unborn baby is a human person, whose rights should also be considered as well as the rights of the mother. Christians would say, yes, unborn babies are human beings. They are made in the image of God and their lives are precious and deserve protection—even if allowing them to live means another person going through the hard process of pregnancy and childbirth. Just as Christians first challenged the idea that it was okay to leave newborn babies out to die, so today, Christians are challenging the idea that it's okay to kill unborn babies in the womb.

Some would say that in the early stages of pregnancy, there isn't a baby, there's just a ball of cells. But if you look at the process of embryo development, there is no clear point at which you could say, "Now this is a human person who deserves protection, where yesterday there was just a ball of cells."

Some people say that babies should count from the time when they could survive outside their mother's womb. But that is after babies can hear and suck their thumbs. And as medicine has advanced, younger and younger babies have been able to survive outside the womb, so it's not a clear, unchanging cut-off point. It would also be a different point for people in different countries, depending on how good the healthcare in that country was.

Others say that a baby should count as a human person only from the time she is born. But an unborn baby in the later stages of pregnancy is no different from a baby born prematurely—like my sixteen-year-old niece, who was born so early that her dad's wedding ring could fit around her upper arm—so saying birth is the dividing line doesn't make sense.

When I was around your age, people who were "pro-choice" argued strongly that killing an unborn baby was *not* like killing a newborn baby. But some people today are arguing that it should be okay to kill a baby even after he or she is born, if the baby is disabled or if the parents just decide they don't want the baby anymore.[4]

Some people think that being against abortion (also known as being "pro-life") means not caring about women. I disagree. Half the babies who die from abortions in the West are baby girls and in China and India—two countries where the teachings of Jesus haven't yet made a big impact on how people think—far more than half the babies who die this way are girls.[5] What's more, as we'll see in chapter 7, sex outside the commitment of marriage, which results in the majority of unplanned pregnancies, tends not to be good for the happiness and well-being of women.

If there is no God making human beings in his image, unborn babies *are* just balls of cells without infinite value. But if there is no God making humans in his image, that is also true of you and me. As Yuval Noah Harari puts it, we don't have rights any more than spiders or hyenas. Or as the character Dr. House put it in the popular TV series *House M.D.*, you're "just a bag of cells and waste with an expiration date."[6]

My friend Sarah Irving-Stonebraker is a history professor at a university in Australia. I met her when we were both doing our

PhDs at Cambridge University. She was a convinced atheist at that time. But when she realized that atheism didn't support her belief in universal human rights or her belief that newborn babies are more valuable than animals, she started to wonder whether atheism was true. As Sarah did more research, she discovered to her surprise that believing in human rights and equality—believing that even the very young, the very poor, and the very sick deserved our care—had come historically from Christianity. So Sarah started considering Christianity for the first time. When Sarah found out the truth about Jesus, her world turned upside down, and she started following him.

What about Enemies?

There's a scene in *Harry Potter and the Deathly Hallows* when Harry and his friends face a hard choice. Harry, Ron, and Hermione are in the "Room of Requirement"—a room that appears when any Hogwarts student needs it. But Harry's worst enemy, Draco Malfoy, is also in the room. One of Malfoy's friends tries to kill Hermione and accidentally starts a cursed fire that spreads like—well—fire through the room. Harry and his friends grab broomsticks to fly out. But then they see that Draco and his friend are stuck. Harry has a choice: fly out of the room to safety or risk his own life to save his enemy. Harry chooses to rescue Malfoy.

Whether you're a follower of Jesus or not, you feel some respect for Harry and his friends in this moment. We wouldn't have blamed them for leaving Malfoy and his nasty friend to die. But we deeply admire them for risking their lives to save their enemies. Have you ever wondered why you think this? The answer, again, is Jesus.

One time, as Jesus was teaching his disciples, he said some earth-shattering, world-changing words:

> You have heard that it was said, "You shall love your neighbor and hate your enemy." But I say to you, Love your enemies and pray for those who persecute you, so that you may be sons of your Father who is in heaven. (Matthew 5:43–45)

It's easy for us to love our friends. It's no surprise that Harry, Ron, and Hermione show up for one another and will even take risks to save each other. Most moral systems are based on the idea that you should love and sacrifice for people on your team. But Jesus turned that idea on its head. He taught that we should love and sacrifice even for people who *hate* us. And Jesus didn't just say this. He did it!

As we saw in chapter 1, when the Roman soldiers had nailed him to the cross, Jesus prayed that God would forgive them (Luke 23:34). What's more, Jesus's *reason* for coming to earth in the first place and dying on the cross was to love his enemies. In a letter to the first Christians in Rome, Paul explains it like this:

> For one will scarcely die for a righteous person—though perhaps for a good person one would dare even to die—but God shows his love for us in that while we were still sinners, Christ died for us. (Romans 5:7–8)

If you're not a follower of Jesus, you might think this sounds weird. We may not believe in Jesus, but we're not his *enemies*! But according to the Bible, we are (Romans 5:10). We've turned away from the God who made us and loves us and gives us everything we have (Romans 3:10–12). That's what it means to be a "sinner."

Like Harry's enemies, we deserve to die in the fire of our own making. But Jesus didn't turn away from us. He didn't even just risk his life, as Harry did. Jesus gave his life on purpose to save us.

Okay, you might say, so maybe Jesus is the reason we think it's not okay to hate people who are different from us. Perhaps he's even the reason we think it's morally good to love and sacrifice for your enemies. He had some great ideas, and maybe he can tell Christians what's right and what's wrong. But why does Jesus get to decide what's right and what's wrong for everyone else? Shouldn't people from different cultures and religions get to decide for themselves what's good and what's bad?

A Terrible Tuesday

On Tuesday September 11, 2001, four US planes were hijacked, as men wielding box cutters took over the different cockpits and started piloting the planes. It's very rare that planes ever get hijacked like this. (You're more likely to be struck by lightning than to be on a plane that gets hijacked.) But on September 11, 2001, four planes were taken over by members of a Muslim terrorist group called Al-Qaeda. The hijackers didn't want money. They wanted to crash the planes into important buildings in New York City and Washington DC. They wanted lots of people to die, and they were willing to die themselves to make that happen.

You can probably imagine someone really bad wanting to murder lots of innocent people. Maybe it would help them become rich or powerful. History is full of examples like this. But the people who hijacked those planes knew they weren't going to become rich or powerful. They knew they were going to die. They crashed the planes because they believed God wanted them to and that he would reward them in the next life. If a soldier gave up his life in an important battle, we might think he was a hero. And while most Muslims in the world—including all my Muslim friends—*disagreed* with what the men who hijacked those planes did, the Muslims in Al-Qaeda celebrated them as heroes. Those men chose to kill and to die, because they believed they were serving their God.

Did those sincere beliefs make what the hijackers did right? Not at all! It was a terrible, terrible thing to do. Thousands of innocent people died. Thousands more were left grieving for their loved ones. But if we say that what's right and what's wrong can change depending on someone's religious beliefs, then we can't say that what those hijackers did was *wrong*. They were simply following what they believed.

So Does Religion Make Things Worse?

When some people look at history and see things like the events of September 11, 2001, they think religion must be the problem. People of all religions, including Christians, have done terrible things in the name of religion. Famous physicist Steven Weinberg said that without religion, "you would have good people doing good things and evil people doing evil things. But for good people to do evil things, that takes religion."[7] September 11 shows that some religious beliefs *can* make people do awful things. So it's easy to think that religion is causing the problem. But if we look at all the evidence, we will discover a different story.

First, we must understand that—while there is sometimes overlap between the moral teachings of different religious traditions—different religions teach different things. In 1948, an international committee published the Universal Declaration of Human Rights, which was meant to be a basic moral code that people of all different religions could agree to uphold. But some majority-Muslim countries would not agree to it, and, in 1982, Iran's representative Said Raja'i Khorasani complained that the declaration was a "secular understanding of the Judeo-Christian tradition" that "could not be implemented by Muslims."[8]

Second, as historian Tom Holland points out, the standards by which even an atheist like Steven Weinberg judges good and evil are ultimately Christian standards: assuming universal human equality; moral responsibility toward even our enemies; a duty of special care toward the poor, weak, and oppressed, etc.

Third, there is evidence to suggest that actively religious people in general treat others better. For example, Americans who go to religious services every week are *less* likely to do bad things (like commit crimes) and *more* likely to do good things (like give money to charity and volunteer to help others) than non-religious Americans.[9]

Fourth, if we look back over the last hundred years, we'll find that many of the most terrible things have been done by people who didn't believe in God at all. For example, people following an atheistic belief system called Communism have ended up killing millions and millions of people in horrible ways. Communist governments in Russia and China killed even more people than the terrible German dictator Adolph Hitler, who was responsible for the killing of six million Jews. In fact, Communist leaders have killed more people than any religious government in history, even though the basic idea at the heart of Communism is the drive to make everyone equal. This isn't just in the past. Right now, the Communist government in China is holding over a million Uighur Muslims in concentration camps like those set up for Jews in Nazi Germany.

What's more, if there *is* no God, we can't even say that killing millions of innocent people is truly, absolutely *wrong*. If there is no God, we are all just bags of cells and waste with an expiration date and there's no such thing as right and wrong: there's only my opinion against yours. When atheist author Richard Dawkins looks at the world, he sees a universe that looks exactly as we'd expect "if there is, at bottom, no design, no purpose, no evil and no good, nothing but blind, pitiless indifference."[10] If he is right and there is no God, then there is no good and there is no evil and human beings don't have rights any more than spiders, hyenas, or chimpanzees.

But if the amazing claims of Jesus are true—if he really is who he says he is—then he's not just a guy who lived two thousand years ago and gave us some great moral teachings. He's also the Creator of the universe. He made the law of gravity, and he made the laws of morality. He made you and he made me—and he's the only one who has the right to say what's right and what's wrong.

If you think about it, that's really good news. Because if no one has the right to say what's evil and what's good—not just for us here, but for people across the world, no matter their beliefs, or culture, or the time at which they live—then we're stuck in the world that's even worse than the moral world of *Wreck-It-Ralph*, where someone who had done terrible things could just say, "I'm bad, and that's good. I will never be good, and that's not bad. There's no one I'd rather be than me."[11] We're stuck in a world where there isn't even good or bad or right or wrong. There's nothing but blind, pitiless indifference.

- Jesus made all lives count, including babies, sick people, poor people, and even our enemies. His moral teachings changed the world.

- If there is no God, then it's true that unborn babies are just a bunch of cells. But if there is no God, then you and I are just bunches of cells too.

- People can do terrible things in the name of God, even sincerely believing that what they are doing is right. But if there is no God, we can't say these things are truly wrong.

- If there is no God who created the universe, there is no universal right and wrong. We can all just have different opinions. But if there is a Creator God, he has the right to tell us what to do.

- While many people have done terrible things in the name of religion, taking religion away doesn't seem to help. Communism— an atheistic belief system that's meant to bring about human equality—has resulted in more deaths in the last hundred years than any other belief system in history.

- In America, people who go to church tend to be more generous to others and less likely to commit crimes than those who don't.

- The basic moral standards by which most of us judge right and wrong today—whether we are Christians or atheists—ultimately came from Christianity. If we take that foundation away, we are left with no right, no wrong, no evil, and no good. In the end, our lives and actions don't matter at all.

How Can You Believe the Bible Is True?

When Aladdin first meets the genie, he mutters to himself in disbelief: "I'm talking to a smoking blue giant?" The genie responds,

> I am not a giant. I am a genie. There's a difference. Giants are not real.[1]

The genie's response is funny because it's absurd. If anything, it's *easier* to believe in an extra-large human than in a magical, wish-granting being that pops out of a lamp! We might enjoy fanciful stories like *Aladdin*, but we don't for a moment think that they're *true*. Some people think we should view the Bible the same way.

The Bible was written thousands of years ago, and it makes some incredible claims. It claims there is a God who made the universe. It claims God sent his Son into the world to die on a cross for people like you and me. It claims that Jesus performed miracles, that he was raised from the dead, that he now lives with all his followers by God's Spirit, and that he will come back to earth one day as universal judge and king. These are extraordinary claims. We'd need some serious evidence to believe them. But they're not claims that only stupid people believe. In fact, some of the smartest people in the world believe that what the Bible says is true.

In this chapter, we'll focus on Jesus himself, and we'll see that there *is* good evidence to believe what the Bible says about him. We'll also see that the Bible speaks truth to us in different ways, and we need to pay careful attention to read it well.

Did Jesus Even Exist?

Some people question whether Jesus even existed. But all serious historians agree that he did. We have evidence from *outside* the Bible—from writings by people who didn't even like Christians— that confirm that Jesus was a first-century, Jewish teacher, that he was crucified by the Romans during the reign of the Emperor Tiberius (who ruled AD 14 to AD 37) and under the authority of Pontius Pilate (who was the governor of Judea between AD 26 and AD 36) and that Christians believed he was the Messiah (God's promised king) and worshiped him. We also have accounts of Jesus's life from the four Gospels (Matthew, Mark, Luke, and John), which include all sorts of accurate details about the time and place in which Jesus lived.[2] Even historians who do not believe in God *at all* agree that Jesus was a real person.

Were the Gospels Written Too Long after Jesus's Life to Be Trusted?

We don't have the first copies of the Gospels. We have copies of copies of copies. But that's not surprising at all. If you've ever learned about Greek and Roman history, most of what you've learned has been based on copies of copies of copies of copies of things people originally wrote down. And we have far more manuscript evidence for the life of Jesus than we do for the lives of many other important historical figures of his time—including the Roman emperor Tiberius who ruled during Jesus's ministry.

When Jesus was born, most people could not read and write. There were no computers or printers or email. Most people learned by listening, and the disciples (or students) of a Jewish teacher would often know all their teachings by heart, like you might know the lyrics of songs by your favorite singer or lines in your favorite movies. (My nineteen-year-old nephew knows all the words to all the songs in *Moana*—don't ask me why!)

Jesus had twelve chosen disciples and lots of other followers who traveled with him. Thousands of people listened to his teaching and saw his miracles. After his resurrection, Jesus told his disciples to spread his message throughout the world (Matthew 28:18–20). At first, they did this just by word of mouth. But when the first witnesses were starting to die out, four accounts of Jesus's life were written down: the Gospels of Matthew, Mark, Luke, and John.

In a book called *Jesus and the Eyewitnesses*, world-class New Testament scholar Richard Bauckham gives us evidence that these Gospels are based on eyewitness accounts. He points out that the writers often mention the names of the people they had talked to, so that anyone reading the Gospels would know whom to ask to test the accuracy of the writing. It would be like saying, "If you don't believe me, go and ask so-and-so: she saw it with her own eyes!"[3] Experts believe that Mark's Gospel was written first, and that it was probably written thirty-five to forty-five years after

Jesus's death. That might sound like a long time to you. But is it too long for us to trust what Mark says about Jesus?

My kids love hearing stories from when my grandpa was young. Their favorite story is of a time when great-grandpa was a kid, and he was in a swimming competition. His nickname was "Mac," and as he swam in a race, his friends shouted, "Come on Mac!" But because he was putting his head in and out of the water as he swam, he thought they were shouting, "Come back!" So he turned around and started swimming back to the start! This happened about seventy years ago. My grandpa told the story to my mum when she was little, and to me when I was little, and now he tells it to my kids. It hasn't changed over time. And it's a story from *twice* as long ago as the time between Jesus's death and when Mark's Gospel was written down.

If your parents are in their thirties or forties, ask them to tell you about something that happened to them when they were kids. Then ask them if they're *sure* it happened, or if that's too long ago for them to remember. Or ask your grandparents to tell you stories about when your parents were little. Because that's about the same time difference between when Jesus was teaching and when the Gospels were written down.

My grandpa's story is funny. But it's not important. The other people there that day probably don't remember the story and probably didn't tell it to their great-grandchildren. But the teachings of Jesus and the things he did were *really* important. Lots of people were watching and listening to Jesus. He changed people's lives and many of those people were willing to face execution for telling others about Jesus. The Gospels were written to make sure that the stories about Jesus would still be told accurately after the eye witnesses had died and could not be consulted anymore. Jesus's followers didn't want the stories about Jesus to be changed. They were too important.

What If People Just Made Up Stories about Jesus?

My daughter has a friend who says his brother can jump off tall buildings and not get hurt. I'm sure he knows this isn't true. He's just saying it to get attention. Some people think that the Gospel writers made up stories about Jesus to get attention too. But there are several problems with this theory.

First, the most crazy-sounding claim in the Gospels is Jesus's resurrection. You might make up that your hero had risen from the dead if you thought you would get lots of attention or make lots of money. But if people might *kill you* for saying that, you'd probably stop, right? Many of Jesus's first followers were beaten and killed for saying that very thing.

Second, the stories in the Gospels are *really* embarrassing for the disciples. Peter was one of Jesus's closest followers and a key leader in the early church. Experts believe that Mark's Gospel was based on Peter's memories of Jesus. Mark tells us that Peter had promised that he'd stick with Jesus even if everyone else ran away (Mark 14:29–31). So far so good for Peter. But Mark also says that on the night that Jesus was arrested, Peter claimed three times that he didn't even know who Jesus was (Mark 14:66–72)! If I were Peter, I wouldn't want people to know that part of the story—unless it really happened, and I thought that telling the truth about Jesus was more important than what people thought of me. I *definitely* wouldn't make it up or let other people make up a story like that and spread it around!

Third, some people argue that as years went by, more and more crazy stories were made up about Jesus. But the earliest writings we have about Jesus (some of the New Testament letters) talk about his resurrection, and this is his most amazing miracle. If people were exaggerating about Jesus over time, you'd expect the most crazy-sounding story to come last. But the resurrection claim is in the earliest writings about Jesus that we have. And if you think about it, if Jesus really was raised from the dead, it's not so crazy to believe that he also healed people, or walked on water, or stopped storms.

But what if the disciples truly *thought* Jesus had been raised to life, but in fact he just hadn't died in the first place?

What If Jesus Didn't Really Die?

In the classic comic film, *The Princess Bride*, the hero Wesley gets tortured to death. But his friends take him to see a man called Miracle Max. After inspecting Wesley's body, Max reassures them:

> It just so happens that your friend here is only *mostly* dead. There's a big difference between *mostly* dead and *all* dead. . . . Mostly dead is *slightly* alive.[4]

By the end of the day, thanks to Max's miracle pill, Wesley is alive enough to fight his enemies.

Some people wonder if Jesus wasn't *all* dead after he was crucified, but just *mostly* dead so that after a few days he revived. But Roman soldiers knew how to kill. In fact, they often had the job of crucifying people who claimed to be God's Messiah. Crucifixion (the method used to kill Jesus) was designed to maximize pain and to leave the victim not just *mostly* dead, but *all* dead.

We saw in chapter 3 that Jesus was either raised from the dead or he was not and that different religions disagree about whether or not he was raised. So is there any evidence to think that Christianity is right and that Jesus truly came back to life?

Is There Any Evidence for the Resurrection?
In March 2020, my kids' school closed because of the coronavirus. Offices closed. Sports games got cancelled. Churches stopped being able to meet. I'm writing this a few months later and at this point, hundreds of thousands of people have died. If you had told me in 2019 that all of this was going to happen, I would not have believed you. It would have sounded too crazy.

The coronavirus seems to have started in one place, but it spread from person to person until it was all over the world. As I'm writing this right now, hundreds of millions of people are living differently because of it. Hundreds of thousands of people have died from it. You can't see the virus itself without a microscope. But the evidence for it is everywhere. The evidence for the resurrection of Jesus is a bit like that. But instead of it being terrible news of death, like the coronavirus, it's the most wonderful news of life.

Jesus's disciples weren't expecting him to be raised. After his crucifixion they were very upset and scared. As we saw earlier, Jesus's most enthusiastic disciple—Peter—was so scared after Jesus was arrested that he couldn't even admit that he knew Jesus. Then three days after Jesus's death, some of his female followers said they'd seen Jesus *alive* (see Matthew 28:1–10; Mark 16:1–11; Luke 24:1–12; John 19:11–18). At that time, people didn't take what women said very seriously, so if you were trying to make up a convincing story, you definitely wouldn't have women be the first witnesses. It would be like making up a story today and saying that you'd heard it from a few young kids. The only reason the

Gospels would say that women were the first witnesses of Jesus's resurrection was if they really were. What's more, if the Roman and Jewish authorities had produced the body of Jesus, they could have proved Jesus hadn't been raised. But they didn't.

Turning a few scared disciples who had abandoned Jesus when danger came into people who were willing to give their lives proclaiming that he had been raised from the dead took a miracle. And that miracle happened. Jesus's male and female followers started passing the message on until it was all around the world. They proclaimed that Jesus had died for our sins, taking the punishment we deserved, and that he had been raised from the dead to give us new life. For the last two thousand years, this new life has been spreading, person to person, as people have heard the good news about Jesus and believed in him. Unlike a virus, this new life can't be seen under a microscope. We can't prove beyond a doubt that the resurrection happened. But we can see the effects of it all over the world. And if you think about it, if there *is* a God who made the universe and gave us life in the first place, it's not crazy to think that God could raise someone from the dead.

The Bible claims that Jesus *literally* rose from the dead. His physical body came back to life. He talked and walked and ate with his disciples, and to be a Christian you need to believe that this is literally true. When I tell people I believe that Jesus was literally raised from the dead, they sometimes ask me if I take the whole of the Bible literally. This is an important question with an interesting answer.

Should We Always Read the Bible Literally?
In *Frozen*, Anna and Hans sing a song called, "Love Is an Open Door" to describe their feelings for each other. For most of her life, her sister

Elsa's door had been shut in Anna's face, but things changed when she met Hans. Anna uses a metaphor (or word picture) to describe how she's feeling. Meeting Hans feels like an open door.

When we talk about things we really care about, we often use metaphors. Just like with literal language, we can use metaphors to tell the truth and we can use them to lie. When Anna sings "Love Is an Open Door," she's telling the truth. But as the film goes on, we discover that Hans was lying. They both use the same metaphor, but one uses it to tell the truth and the other uses it to lie. You can use literal language to lie or tell the truth too. Whether we are using a metaphor or literal language to speak doesn't change the truth of what we're saying. It just changes how we're saying it.

If we read the Gospels, we'll find that Jesus often packaged truth in metaphors. For example, Jesus said, "I am the good shepherd. The good shepherd lays down his life for his sheep" (John 10:11). Jesus wasn't *literally* a shepherd, and he wasn't going to die for a bunch of furry animals. No, his people are the sheep, and he cares for us like a shepherd who loves his sheep so much that he'd die to protect them.

Jesus said, "I am the bread of life; whoever comes to me shall not hunger, and whoever believes in me shall never thirst" (John 6:35). He's not literally bread or water. But coming to him is as vital to our lives as eating and drinking.

Jesus said to his disciples, "I am the vine; you are the branches" (John 15:5). Jesus isn't *literally* a plant! He's telling his followers that they are so deeply connected to him that they're like the branches of a vine. There are many other examples of Jesus using metaphors to tell us the truth, so when we are reading the Bible, we need to have our antennae out for metaphors.

Jesus also told lots of stories. The parable of the good Samaritan (which we mentioned in chapter 2) is one example (Luke 10:25–37). It's a story about a man who was beaten up on the road from Jerusalem to Jericho. Jesus didn't tell the story because it *literally* happened. He told it as an example to teach us that loving your neighbor includes loving strangers from different racial, cultural, and religious backgrounds—even those we might see as enemies.

Most of the time, it's obvious when the Bible is speaking truth to us through metaphors or parables, and it's important that we read different parts of the Bible differently. For instance, the book of Psalms is a collection of poem-songs, and you wouldn't read a poem the same way you'd read a history book. In a few places, Christians disagree about whether a part of the Bible should be read literally or not. It isn't *always* easy to tell. But mostly it is.

Understanding that the Bible often teaches us through stories and metaphors doesn't mean we can say that any part of the Bible we find difficult to believe is a story or a metaphor. As we have already seen, the Bible is clear that Jesus was *literally* raised from the dead. You can't be a follower of Jesus if you don't believe this. What's more, Jesus uses metaphors to teach some of the hardest truths. For example, when he said,

> Enter by the narrow gate. For the gate is wide and the way is easy that leads to destruction, and those who enter by it are many. For the gate is narrow and the way is hard that leads to life, and those who find it are few. (Matthew 7:13–14)

So when people ask me, "Do you take the Bible literally?" I don't just answer yes or no. I explain that some parts of the Bible are not *meant* to be taken literally. But then I explain that there are many parts of the Bible that are: for example, the claim that Jesus literally rose from the dead.

Can Really Intelligent People Believe the Bible?

My friend Roz Picard is a professor at MIT, one of the top universities for science in the world. She's a computer scientist, and she designs amazing robots that can recognize and copy human emotions. When Roz was a teenager, she was a "proud atheist," and she thought the Bible was "full of fantastical crazy stuff." Then a friend challenged her to read the Bible for herself. As the Bible is the best-selling book of all time, she decided to try. As she read, she was surprised: "I started reading the Bible," Roz recalls, "and it started to change me." She ended up being convinced that Jesus truly is the Son of God, who died so she could live.

My friend Ian Hutchinson is also an MIT professor. Like Roz, he wasn't raised as a Christian. He became a Christian when he was in college, after some of his highly intelligent friends told him about Jesus. In 2018, he wrote a book called *Can a Scientist Believe in Miracles?* in which he answers dozens of questions about Christianity that he's been asked by students over the years.[5] His answer to one of the most important questions in the book— "Can a scientist believe in the resurrection?"—is absolutely yes!

Believing the Bible isn't just for stupid people. It isn't like believing in genies or giants. Some of the smartest people in the world believe the Bible, including professors of science, history, philosophy, and theology. In fact, like the first disciples who shared the message of Jesus, they'd stake their lives on it.

- Whatever their personal beliefs, historians agree that Jesus was a real person. Non-Christian sources from the first century confirm that Jesus was a Jewish teacher who was believed to be the Messiah, crucified by the Romans between AD 26 and AD 36, and worshiped like a god.
- The Gospel accounts of Jesus's life that we have in the New Testament were written well within the living memory of eyewitnesses and include many specific details about the place and culture in which Jesus lived.
- It's hard to believe that Jesus's first followers made up the stories about him. Some of the stories in the Gospels are very embarrassing for the first Christian leaders. They wouldn't have made those stories up and they wouldn't have been willing to die proclaiming that Jesus had been raised from the dead when they knew that was a lie.
- While we can't prove beyond reasonable doubt that Jesus really was raised from death, alternative explanations (for example, that he didn't really die, or that the story of the resurrection was just made up) make very little sense.
- It took a miracle to turn a handful of scared disciples into people who started a movement that changed the world.
- If there is a God who made the universe, it's not crazy to think that he might have raised Jesus from the dead.
- Reading the Bible faithfully doesn't always mean reading it literally. Jesus himself often used nonliteral language (metaphors and stories) to tell us important truths. But there are many parts of the

Bible that clearly are meant to be read literally: for example, the claim that Jesus literally rose from the dead.

- Some of the smartest people in the world—including people who know all about modern science—believe that the Bible is true.

Hasn't Science Disproved Christianity?

When Moana meets the demigod Maui, he thinks she's come as a fangirl. He sings the famous song, "You're Welcome" and boasts about his role in creating the world in which Moana lives. In fact, he claims to be able to "explain every natural phenomenon," including the sun, the ground, the sky, the tides—even the origin of coconut trees—with stories of his own exploits.[1] Moana is not impressed. And many of my friends are not impressed with such creation stories either. They prefer to explain natural phenomena with science.

Many people today see believing in science as the *opposite* of believing stories about creation. *Once upon a time* (they think) *people had to make up myths to explain how the world around them came to be. But now we have science; we don't need stories anymore.*

The Bible begins with the story of God creating the world—from stars to starfish. Do we still need this story? Isn't science based on *not* believing in a Creator God? Haven't Christians always been against science? These are some of the questions we'll look at in this chapter. You might be surprised by the answers.

One God

Every ancient culture had ways of explaining the natural world, usually involving gods or demigods (like Maui) acting in human-like ways. In some creation stories, the world came from fights between gods. In some, humans were created to be slaves. But the creation story found in the book of Genesis at the beginning of the Bible is unique: rather than seeing the world as a result of many gods—or even one main god versus others—the Bible claims that there is only one God, who made the heavens and the earth. He created with his words and he made humans "in his own image" (Genesis 1:27).

Most people in the world identify as either Christian, Muslim, or Jewish—and all of these three religions teach that there is only one God. But when the first book of the Bible was written, most people believed in *lots* of gods. The idea that there was only one Creator God would have sounded as strange to them as the idea of many gods sounds to us. But the biblical claim that there is only one God who created the world and made humans in his image is the basis for many things we take for granted today—including what we now call "science."

Christians Invented Modern Science

Rather than science being the opposite of belief in God, the first modern scientists invented the scientific method because they believed in the Creator God of the Bible, who is totally in charge, incredibly intelligent, and completely free. (Fun fact: two of the guys who helped develop the scientific method had the last name Bacon!)

Scientists try to figure out the laws that run the universe. First, they notice something happening in nature, and they ask, "Why is that happening?" Next, they come up with a theory called a *hypothesis* to explain why that thing might be happening. Then they test that hypothesis by running experiments. Scientists assume that everything in nature is caused by something else, and that the cause-and-effect will work the same way wherever you are in the world, because the universe follows consistent rules.

Today, we are so used to this scientific process that we don't question it. But the first scientists believed there were consistent laws running the universe because they believed that there was a consistent, law-giving God. They learned from the Bible that there was only one God, who created the universe in an orderly way, and that he was the kind of God who didn't change his mind. So they guessed that he'd made the universe according to laws that would work the same all over the world and wouldn't change over time.

If there were lots of gods, you might expect to find different rules in different places (a bit like different countries having different laws), and you might expect the rules to change depending on which god was in charge in that place or at that time. But if there is only one God over the whole world—who has always been in charge and will always be in charge—you would expect the laws to be the same in every place and at every time. The first scientists also knew from the Bible that God is completely free: no one tells God what to do. So the only way to find out what laws God put in place was to go and look!

The guy who first explained this to me is a philosophy professor at Princeton University named Hans Halvorson. Hans is one of the top experts on thinking about science in the world. He is also a Christian. Hans explains that people started doing science because they believed in the God of the Bible, and that even today, people who believe in a Creator God have a better reason for doing science than atheists do. You see, if you *don't* think there's a God who made the laws of the universe in the first place—if you believe the universe is here by accident, for no reason at all—then there's no final explanation for why science works. You just have to say, "Aren't we lucky that it does work?"[2]

Of course, there are lots of great scientists who don't believe in God. In fact, professional scientists today are significantly *less* likely than non-scientists to believe in God—perhaps because so many people think that faith in God is contrary to science. But there are also many world-class scientists today who *do* believe in God. What's more, if we look back over the last four hundred years, we'll see that Christians have played an important role in many groundbreaking scientific discoveries—including developing an amazing explanation for how the universe itself began.

The Birth of the Universe

Almost a century ago, a Roman Catholic priest named Georges Lemaître proposed a crazy-sounding theory. Most scientists in his day believed the universe had always existed. But Lemaître's hypothesis was that it had a beginning. He suggested that the whole universe had started off as an incredibly hot, incredibly dense point (which he called a "cosmic egg") and that it had expanded from there with unbelievable speed. Imagine holding an egg in your hands. And then imagine that the entire universe was packed into that egg. It sounds more crazy than a genie coming out of a lamp! But thousands of scientists have done thousands of experiments to confirm that the so-called "Big Bang" theory really does seem to describe what happened.

When Georges Lemaître developed the idea, many scientists didn't believe it. It sounded ridiculous. It also sounded too much like what the Bible says about God creating the universe out of nothing. In fact, some atheist scientists at the time tried to prove it wasn't true, because they didn't like it—including a physicist named Fred Hoyle, who came up with the term "Big Bang" to mock Lemaître's idea. If you read popular atheist authors like Richard Dawkins, you'll get the idea that science has replaced belief in God and that Christians have always fought against science. The history of the Big Bang theory tells us the opposite story.

We've seen already that Christians *invented* modern science, and one of the first people to figure out how the universe began was a Christian. But is it *mostly* true that Christians have been against science? Let's do what scientists do and test that hypothesis.

Galileo

Atheist authors often point to Galileo as a great example of Christians rejecting science. For centuries, scientists had taught that the sun revolved around the earth, basing their understanding on the work of the ancient Greek philosopher Aristotle. Galileo was one of the first people to argue that, in fact, the earth revolved around the sun. In 1633, Galileo was found guilty of heresy (believing or teaching things against the Bible) by the Catholic church. Many people today believe that Galileo was tortured by the church and that this is a perfect example of Christians opposing science's progress because they want to take the Bible literally. But there are several problems with this version of the Galileo story.

First, Galileo was a Christian himself, so this is not a story of an atheist scientist being opposed by Christians. Galileo argued that the idea of the earth rotating around the sun did not go against the Bible. In fact, daring to make a theological argument was part of what got him in trouble with the pope (the head of the Catholic church) who had originally supported his scientific work.

Second, Galileo was not imprisoned and tortured by the Catholic church. That is a widely believed myth. He was confined to his house, but not sent to prison and there is no evidence that he was tortured.

Third, as Galileo himself pointed out, Christians had been reading parts of the Bible non-literally for hundreds of years before he suggested the earth went around the sun. In fact, Aristotle's model, which the church had endorsed before scientists like Galileo proposed a different model, also would not fit with a strictly literal understanding of the Bible, which talks about the earth being immovable (e.g., Psalm 93:1) and set on pillars (1 Samuel 2:8). But this is not a problem with the Bible. The Psalms use metaphors all the time, and if you read Hannah's song in 1 Samuel 2, you'll see her using metaphors as well.

Rather than the story of Galileo being a Christians-versus-scientists story, therefore, it's a story about a Christian scientist arguing with other Christians about science and the Bible. And if you study the history of science, you'll find that in all the famous "science versus Christianity" stories, there are actually Christians on both sides of the argument.

Einstein's Heroes

Albert Einstein was a brilliant physicist and one of the most famous scientists of the twentieth century. Einstein was not a Christian, but he kept pictures of his top three scientist heroes on the wall of his study. All of them (Isaac Newton, Michael Faraday, and James Clerk Maxwell) were passionate believers in God.

Isaac Newton (ca. 1642–1727) is one of the most influential scientists of all time. He figured out the basic laws of gravity and motion. Although he didn't believe that Jesus was fully God (which is key to authentic Christianity), he deeply believed that God had created the universe, and he wrote more about God than about science!

Michael Faraday (1791–1867) is one of the greatest experimental scientists ever and is best known for his work on electromagnetism. Having something in science named after you is a big deal and the Faraday constant, the Faraday effect, Faraday's law of induction, and Faraday's laws of electrolysis are all named after Michael Faraday. He was a passionate Christian, deeply interested in the relationship between science and faith.

James Clerk Maxwell (1831–1879) was another amazing scientist who figured out connections between electricity, magnetism, and light. He was an evangelical Presbyterian, who became an elder in the Church of Scotland. By the time he was around your age, he'd already learned large portions of the Bible by heart.

Einstein's heroes weren't the only believers in God who were amazing scientists. There are many other examples from history, including Robert Boyle (1627–1691), who was one of the founders of modern chemistry; Gregor Mendel (1822–1884), who studied pea plants and started the field of science now called genetics; Lord Kelvin (1824–1907), who was one of the first scientists to realize that the earth is really, really, really old; and George Washington Carver (1860s–1943), a pioneering American agricultural chemist, agronomist, and botanist, whose work radically changed the agricultural economy of the US and whose achievements were all the more amazing, as his parents had been enslaved.

But what about today? Can leading scientists be Christians today? Absolutely!

Some Leading Christian Scientists Today

Dr. Francis Collins is one of the most influential scientists in the world today. He led the team that first decoded human DNA (the instruction script in our cells that tells our bodies how to grow). He is now the head of the US National Institutes of Health and oversaw the effort to find a vaccine for the coronavirus. Dr. Collins was not raised as a Christian, and he identified as an atheist when he was a student at Yale University. But after university, he became a hospital doctor, and seeing so many people suffer and die got him thinking about what life really means. He ended up becoming a Christian, after one of his patients told him about her faith in Jesus and asked him, "Doctor, what do you believe?"[3]

Joan Centrella is Deputy Director of Astrophysics Research at NASA. She is a world expert on black holes—some of the most mysterious things in our universe! Centrella became a Christian when she was already a top scientist. She considered different religions before deciding which one to believe: "I chose to follow Christ," she says, "because his words impressed me as being true in a very fundamental way."[4]

MIT professor Jing Kong grew up as an atheist in China. She became a Christian when she was a grad student at Stanford. Now she is a professor of electrical engineering. "My research is only a platform for me to do God's work," she says. "His creation, the way he made this world. . . . It's amazing, really."[5]

Daniel Hastings (whom we met in chapter 1) is a world expert in space science and a professor of aeronautics and astronautics at MIT. He became a Christian when he was a teenager in England. "I start by saying there is a God who created the universe," Hastings says, "and he is not an impersonal God. He has declared Himself as a loving God, who seeks a relationship with us. . . . Our purpose is found in relationship with Him."[6]

Russell Cowburn is a physics professor at Cambridge University. He's a world expert in nanotechnology, which means extremely tiny technology! But the more he studies really small things, the more he believes in a really big God. "Understanding more of science doesn't make God smaller," he explains. "It allows us to see His creative activity in more detail."[7]

Across the world today, there are thousands of Christians who are experts in all sorts of scientific fields. Like the first scientists, they don't see science as an alternative hypothesis to God. Instead, they see their study of science as worship. As pioneering astronomer Johannes Kepler put it, when we study the laws underlying God's universe we are sharing in God's thoughts.[8]

But it is also true that there have been times in the last four hundred years (since modern science started) when Christians have resisted scientific discoveries because they thought the story of science conflicted with the story of the Bible. Let's look at the most famous instance of this conflict.

What about Human Origins?

One of the hot spots in the perceived conflict between science and Christianity is around the question of how human beings came to exist. The Bible says that God made us humans "in his own image" (Genesis 1:27), gave us the special role of ruling over his creation, and called us to a special relationship with him—different from his relationship with any other creature. But in 1859, a British scientist named Charles Darwin published a book called *On the Origin of Species*, in which he argued that all living beings are related to each other, and that human beings had gradually "evolved" from other animals.

Christians in Darwin's day disagreed about whether his scientific theory could fit with the Bible's account of creation. Some argued that the Bible describes God creating humans from the dust of the earth, but that there's no reason he couldn't have created humans gradually through an evolutionary process while still making human beings special. Others argued that evolution doesn't fit with a more literal reading of the biblical creation story and therefore believed that God created humans suddenly and not gradually. As we saw in chapter 5, Christians disagree about how we should understand some parts of the Bible, and the creation accounts in Genesis 1 and 2 are an important example of this type of disagreement.

Today, as in Darwin's day, some Christians think that you can't believe in evolution *and* believe that God created us, while other

Christians think you can. Some argue that Christians should believe God used evolution to create humans, but that he intervened at stages in the process, so we should expect to find some elements in the story of human origins that cannot be explained by science. Others argue that God is in charge of the whole process, so we don't need to look for evidence of his action in the parts we can't explain, because he is directing every tiny step. It's also worth noting that while scientists have a theory to explain how more complex life forms developed from simpler ones, they really don't know how life got started in the first place!

Atheist authors like Richard Dawkins tend to add in all sorts of other beliefs when they talk about science, to make it sound like any time we find a possible scientific explanation of something in the natural world, this squeezes God out of the picture. But as we saw earlier in this chapter, Christians first developed science not because they didn't believe God created the world, but because they did. Just as with any other scientific field, there have always been Christians leading in this area of science.[9] But we also shouldn't assume that everything a scientist says is true—partly because, as science advances, what most scientists believe can change (like it did with the Big Bang) and partly because scientists sometimes make it sound like their science has proved what they do or don't believe about God, when it hasn't.

If you're a follower of Jesus, I hope you'll keep exploring and make your mind up for yourself. These questions are definitely complicated. Christian beliefs about how the Bible fits with science aren't like an on-off light switch (yes or no). They're more like the reading lights my girls have attached to their beds, which have multiple buttons you can press to get different levels of brightness and different kinds of color. But any Christian—whatever he or she believes about science—must believe that God created us, that the Bible tells us the most important truths about human beings, and that a scientific description of a human could never give us the full story. This is a place where Christians and atheists most deeply disagree.

What Is a Human Being?

When the brilliant physicist Stephen Hawking was twenty-one, he was diagnosed with motor neuron disease: a terrible illness that gradually broke his body down. Hawking eventually had to use a motorized wheelchair to get around and a specially designed computer to help him speak and write. His daily life depended on computers. But in an interview toward the end of his life, he went one step further: "I regard the brain as a computer which will stop working when its components fail," Hawking said. "There is no heaven or afterlife for broken down computers; that is a fairy story for people afraid of the dark."[10]

Hawking believed that his brain was just a computer. He did not think he was made in the image of God. He thought he was just a complex machine. In his opinion, the specially designed computer attached to his wheelchair that allowed him to speak and the brain-computer in his head that allowed him to think weren't fundamentally different. When he died, he thought, it was going to be just like a computer breaking down.

Many atheist scientists think this way. They believe the only *real* truth is truth we can measure with the tools of science. Oxford physics professor and Christian believer Ard Louis calls this way of thinking, "nothing buttery," because people will say we're "nothing but" what science can describe.[11] So has science shown that we are "nothing but" the things science can measure? Not at all.

As we have seen already, the people who first invented modern science believed in a God who created the universe and could not be measured by science himself. And just because we can study the physical features of a human by using scientific tools does not mean we can understand everything about humans through those tools. MIT professor Ian Hutchinson agrees that he is a complicated biochemical machine, made up of atoms and molecules and all sorts of things we can investigate with the tools of science. But he says he is also a husband, a father, and a sinner saved by God's grace, and these different kinds of descriptions don't have to push each other out.[12] They can all be true at the same time. If one of his kids said to him, "You're not my father! You're just a bunch of atoms and molecules!" we'd think that kid was confused. But we'd also think he was confused if he said the opposite: "You're my dad: you're not atoms and molecules!" If we think about it, we're used to understanding that there's more going on in any situation than science can describe.

Imagine you were watching a football game on TV, but instead of the commentators talking about plays and scores, they were commenting on what was happening scientifically. "One somewhat hairy mammal (height: 6 ft., 2 in., weight: 195 lbs.) extends a limb at velocity 30 mph. Limb collides with ball (weight: 16 oz.), and ball leaves ground at velocity of 15 mph, angle from the ground 30 degrees . . ." You can imagine the commentary going on and on, with more and more scientifically measurable details. These statements could all be true. But no one would watch that TV channel, because the *point* of football is not the scientific details. It's the game!

Likewise, if someone asked me to tell them about my husband, I wouldn't give his height and weight and blood pressure. I'd tell them about his personality, his interests, and the things that make him laugh or cry. Science can tell us many useful and important things, but it can't tell us the most important truths. Science can measure how fast my heart is pumping blood around my body, but you can't use a stethoscope to measure how much I love my husband.

So What?

Stephen Hawking thought that heaven was a "fairy story for people afraid of the dark." If we *only* believe in science, as he did, we don't just lose the hope of life *after* death. We lose the meaning of life *before* death as well.

I'm writing this book on a laptop computer. My one-year-old son is lying next to me, asleep. If I threw my computer out of the window it would be a waste of money. But I could buy a replacement. If I threw my son out of the window, I would be doing something deeply and profoundly wrong. My son is not replaceable, like a computer. He's a unique and precious being, made in the image of God.

Science is an amazing tool. It helps us to discover useful things to make our lives better and to recognize beautiful things about our world. But if we boil everything down to what science can measure, then you and I don't matter anymore. We're just computers in a fleshy case. Believing that God created the universe isn't illogical or outdated. It's not like believing the stories Maui makes up in *Moana*. According to some of the top thinkers in science today, believing in the God of the Bible is the best foundation for science. It's also our best foundation for understanding what a human being is, and why you, and I, and my little baby, Luke, are infinitely valuable.

- Christians first developed modern science, not as an alternative hypothesis to a Creator God but *because* they believed in the God of the Bible, who is both rational and free.
- Scientific explanations don't squeeze God out. They give us a chance to share in God's thoughts as we understand his creation better.
- Christians have always been leaders in science, both in history and today.
- Christians have always been on both sides of debates that people think of as "science versus Christianity," including the controversies about Galileo, Darwin, and the beginning of the universe.
- Science can tell us many amazing and important things, but it can't tell us the most important things about who we are and why we matter.

Why Can't We Just Agree That Love Is Love?

At the climax of *Frozen*, Anna's body is becoming ice. She's been told that "an act of true love" can thaw a frozen heart, so she rushes back to her fiancé, Hans, expecting that a kiss will do the trick. But to her horror, Hans turns out to be a villain. Reeling from this shock, Anna realizes that Kristoff, not Hans, is the man who truly loves her, so she staggers out into the cold to find him. But then Anna sees Hans about to murder her sister. Anna has a choice to make: save herself or save her sister. She rushes to protect Elsa and turns to ice just as Hans's sword falls. But as Elsa weeps over her sister's frozen body, Anna thaws. The act of true love that could thaw Anna's heart was not a kiss from Hans or Kristoff, as she'd thought. It was Anna's *own* act of love: sacrificing herself to save her sister.

In this chapter, we're going to look at the popular claim that "Love is love." When people say this, they mean everyone should be allowed to date and marry whomever they like, regardless of whether they are male or female. This message seems so powerful. We all know love is good, and that the more love there is in the world the better. But as *Frozen* beautifully depicts, there are different *kinds* of love. Powerful, life-changing, self-sacrificing love need not be sexual or romantic. Sister love and brother love, parent and child love, friend-to-friend love all matter too. But according to the Bible, the most powerful love of all is the love that comes from the heart of God himself. In fact, the Bible tells us not that "Love is love," but that "God is love" (1 John 4:8), and that we get glimpses of God's love through different *kinds* of relationships.

Windows into Love

We saw in chapter 2 that God created human beings in his image, and that he designed us for relationship with him and with each other. And just as we can see different rooms of a house when we look through different windows, God planned for us to see different aspects of his love through different kinds of human relationships.

For example, the idea of God as Father springs out of the Old Testament where God talks about his people, Israel, as his son (e.g., Deuteronomy 32:6; Isaiah 63:16–17; Hosea 11:1–4). Then, in the New Testament, Jesus calls God his Father and tells his followers to do the same (Matthew 6:9). If you have a wonderful dad, who cares for you deeply and would do anything to keep you safe, that's a window into one aspect of God's love. But the great news is this: if you *don't* have a loving father, the Bible says that God loves you more than any human father ever could!

The Bible also gives us glimpses of God's love through mothers. For example, in the book of Isaiah, God asks if a woman could forget the baby she is breastfeeding. The obvious answer is, "No way!" But then God says that *even if a mother could* forget her baby, he will never forget his people (Isaiah 49:15). If you have a mother who loves you with her whole heart and would *never* forget you, whatever happened, that's a window into God's love for you. And if you *don't* have a mother who loves you like that, God loves you more than any mother ever could!

Father love and mother love are two important, powerful kinds of love. They are loves that keep us alive as babies and shape us as we grow to adulthood. But they are not romantic or sexual loves. This is one important way in which the "Love is love" message doesn't stand up: parent-child love is vital. Without it, children wouldn't survive. But it's vitally different from sexual and romantic love.

So what about sexual and romantic love: the kind of love that pulls people toward marriage? Well, just as God made fatherhood and motherhood to tell us the story of his love for his people, so he made male and female, sex and marriage, to tell us the story of Jesus's love for his church.

The Love Story

At the beginning of the Bible, we see God creating humans, male and female, in his image and designing them for relationship with him and with each other. Genesis tells us that when a man and a woman get married they become "one flesh" (Genesis 2:24). As the story of the Bible unfolds, we start to see this picture of marriage being used as a metaphor for God's relationship with his people. Old Testament prophets compare God to a faithful husband and God's people (the Israelites) to a wife (e.g., Isaiah

54:5–8; Jeremiah 3:20; Ezekiel 16; Hosea 1:2). God desperately loves his people. But his people keep cheating on him by worshiping other so-called gods. Time after time, God forgives Israel and welcomes her back. But it doesn't seem like this marriage is going to work: a holy God just cannot live with sinful people.

Then Jesus comes.

We saw in chapter 3 that Jesus made extraordinary claims about himself. One of Jesus's amazing claims is that he is "the bridegroom" (Luke 5:34). Jesus took on God's role as husband. God's marriage to his people in the Old Testament didn't work because his people kept sinning and running away from him. But Jesus came to pay the price for sin, so that his people could finally be with him forever. In fact, as we read on in the New Testament, we find that God's plan for marriage *from the very first* was for it to give us a picture of how much Jesus loves us.

Paul explains in a letter to one of the first churches that Christian marriage is meant to give us a glimpse of Jesus's love (Ephesians 5:22–33). Jesus loves and sacrifices for his people; he went to the cross to die for us! Husbands are meant to love their wives like that: "Husbands, love your wives, as Christ loved the church and gave himself up for her" (Ephesians 5:25). This is an amazing call. A husband could only do this with Jesus's help, and even the best human husband will never fully measure up. But a really wonderful husband who loves his wife and is willing to give up everything for her gives us a little window into Jesus's love.

What about wives?

In this picture, the wife plays the part of God's people, who gladly submit to Jesus and follow his lead: "Wives, submit to your own husbands, as to the Lord. For the husband is the head of the wife even as Christ is the head of the church, his body, and is himself its Savior" (Ephesians 5:22–23). The call on wives to submit to their husbands isn't because women are somehow inferior to men, just as the call on husbands to give up their lives for their wives isn't because men are less valuable than women. It also doesn't mean that all women should submit to all men, or that a wife should never say no to her husband if he is treating her badly. In fact, a husband abusing his wife is the total *opposite* of the picture the Bible gives us, where husbands are called again and again to love their wives (Ephesians 5:25, 28, 33; Colossians 3:19) and to understand and honor them (1 Peter 3:7).

The call for husbands and wives to play different roles in Christian marriage is not because men are smarter than women, or because women need more love than men, but because Jesus and the church play different roles in the much greater marriage to which human marriage points. It's like two actors taking different parts in a play.

God made us so that men and woman have different bodies, picturing the radical difference between Jesus and us. But he also made us so that men and women's bodies could fit together in a life-giving closeness, which gives us a picture of Jesus and his church. Paul quotes from the Bible story about the first human couple to make his point: "Therefore a man shall leave his father and his mother and hold fast to his wife, and they shall become one flesh" (Genesis 2:24; Ephesians 5:31). Paul says this "one flesh" reality is a deep mystery and that it's about Christ and the church. In that picture, every believer (male or female) is part of Christ's bride and a member of Christ's body.

I know this all sounds weird! Jesus is one human, but he said he was the bridegroom for *all* God's people, and that means all

God's people form one body together. These are metaphors, like the idea of God as our Father. But as we saw in chapter 5, the Bible often packages the most important truths in metaphors. And the idea that if we trust in Jesus, we are united to him like a husband and a wife, or like a head and a body, is one of the most important truths in the Bible.

A Whole New World

When Jasmin and Aladdin fly on the magic carpet, they sing a song called "A Whole New World," about how their love has changed everything. We search so hard for romantic love, because we think it will change the world for us. A good marriage is a wonderful thing. But if you think (as I did when I was your age) that getting married will change your world and make all your problems go away, you're going to be disappointed. Marriage is not a destination; it's a signpost. At its best, marriage points us to the life-changing closeness of being with Jesus. But our sense that romantic love should make a whole new world is not completely wrong.

In the last book of the Bible, we see the marriage of Jesus and his church bringing heaven and earth back together (see Revelation 19:7; 21:1–5). A human marriage can't remake the world. But the wedding of Jesus to his church will literally begin a whole new, never-ending world, and we can be part of that new world, if we're trusting in him.

So what does all of this mean for human relationships?

A Good Gift in the Wrong Place

Last weekend, I went camping with my family. After dinner, we built a campfire and toasted s'mores. My ten-year-old daughter especially enjoyed learning how to build a fire. But while a campfire in a clearing is a wonderful thing, what would have happened if my daughter had come home and built a campfire in the living room?

The Bible teaches that sex between a man and a woman is a wonderful gift from God and an important part of marriage (1 Corinthians 7:3–5). Sex can bring joy and create life. But like a campfire in the living room, sex can also bring terrible hurt and heartbreak.

As we grow up, our bodies and our hearts can pull us toward others in powerful ways. The films and songs we enjoy often suggest that we should try out sex with different people to find out which person suits us best: like trying on different clothes until you find the perfect fit. But experts have interviewed thousands of people to find out whether having lots of sexual relationships has made them happy, and it turns out that, in general, it doesn't. A loving marriage tends to make both men and women happier. But having sexual relationships with lots of different people tends to make us *less* happy. Like eating too much candy, it might feel good in the moment, but the after-effects can be miserable. According to the research, this is especially true for women.[1] God created sex to go with deep, lifelong commitment, and researchers have found that having sex with just one person consistently does correlate with happiness.[2] But when we pull sex and commitment apart, it hurts.

When I was in college, people thought it was really weird that I wasn't planning to have sex with anyone before I got married (if I did). But as I talked more with other women about this, they would often tell me privately they wished they had made the same decision. The different relationships they'd been in hadn't brought them the happiness they had expected and had often left them feeling empty. One friend I met later shared the same thing. After years of sleeping with different guys, she realized that the lifestyle was making her truly unhappy. She felt like she had to suit up in emotional armor and pretend she didn't care. I told her about the research showing that having sex with lots of different people generally makes people *less* happy. She felt frustrated and asked, "Why wasn't I told this in high school?"

Some of my friends have had even worse experiences. Some have been forced to have sex when they didn't want to. Others had their bodies touched in sexual ways by adults when they were kids. This can happen to boys as well as girls, and often it's done by someone the kid trusts: maybe even a family member. If you've experienced this, I'm so sorry. What has happened to you is not okay, and *it is not your fault*. People who abuse young people in this way usually tell the person they've abused to keep it secret, or make that person think it's their fault, so the victim will feel ashamed and not tell anyone. Sometimes the victims worry that if they did tell someone, they wouldn't be believed. If that's how you feel, you're not alone. Please tell a grown-up you trust and get help.[3] You are not betraying the person who did this to you by telling. You are actually helping them too. Letting someone do something terribly wrong is very bad for them, as well as for the people they are hurting. Sexual touching between adults and kids is the opposite of God's design. It breaks God's heart.

But what about people who are both adults and who want to make a lifelong commitment to each other in marriage, but just happen to be two women or two men? Why would God say no to that?

A Bit about Me

When I was a kid, I wanted to get married someday. The books I read and the songs I heard all pointed to one thing: falling in love was the path to happiness. But I had a problem: the people I found myself dreaming of were girls. I kept hoping I'd grow out of it. When I turned eighteen and went to college, I thought that surely then I'd start liking boys. But right away, I fell in love with a girl again. I couldn't shake it.

You may not relate to that at all. Maybe you have only ever felt attracted to the opposite sex, or perhaps you haven't felt much drawn to either girls or boys yet, except as friends. But if you're thinking, "I'm like that!" you're not alone. A professor named Lisa Diamond at the University of Utah has found that about 14 percent of women and 7 percent of men experience same-sex attraction at least sometimes. This means that if you have ten friends, it's likely that one of them will experience same-sex attraction.

Many people assume that our attractions are something we're just born with and they never change: you're either "gay" or "straight." But Professor Diamond has found that it's much more complicated. First, while 14 percent of women and 7 percent of men experience significant same-sex attraction, only 1 percent of women and 2 percent of men are *only ever* attracted to other women or other men.[4] She has also found that people's feelings can change over time. Many people have the same patterns of attraction throughout their lives. But some people start off feeling attracted to girls and then later find themselves attracted to boys, or vice versa.

I've been happily married to a man for thirteen years. But that's not because my attractions changed. If I'm ever attracted to someone outside my marriage, it's always to a woman. But I'm not in the 1 percent of women who can *only* be attracted to other women. So I'm able to be happily married to a man, and just like any other married Christian, when I find myself attracted to someone other than my husband, I need to ask Jesus for help not to follow that pull.

For many Christians who experience same-sex attraction, however, getting married is not the right choice. For example, my friend Lou started being attracted to other boys when he was a young teenager. As an adult man, he has found he's in the 2 percent of men who are really only attracted to other men, so he has remained single.

But why should being a Christian make a difference? Why shouldn't I have married a woman? Why shouldn't my friend Lou just marry a man? What does the Bible have to say about these questions? One of my best friends found out the answer when she was in college.

A Surprising Story

Rachel grew up in a non-religious home. When she was fifteen, she found herself attracted to a beautiful high school senior girl. She pursued this girl and started a sexual relationship. It felt so right. But the relationship was on and off, and she tried out sleeping with other girls and with boys as well. Rachel found that she was much more attracted to girls, and when she settled back into her relationship with her first girlfriend it felt great. What's more, she had been accepted at Yale—one of the top universities in America. Her life was going so well! Until disaster struck: her girlfriend broke up with her.

Rachel thought that Christians were dumb. But in the hopelessness of having lost the girl she loved, she started wondering if maybe there was a God after all. She googled religious words to see what she could find out. When she started reading about Jesus, she was embarrassed by how much she liked him. Jesus in the Bible seemed so different from the Jesus she'd thought Christians followed. For one thing, he was amazingly clever. But Rachel had heard that Christians were against gay marriage so she worried that saying yes to Jesus would mean saying no to sexual relationships with women.

Rachel asked some friends who identified as Christians and they told her that she didn't have to choose. They said it had all been a misunderstanding and that if Rachel read the Bible rightly, she'd find it *didn't* say that she couldn't marry a woman someday. But when Rachel looked at the Bible passages they were quoting, she could see it wasn't true. She found that the Bible makes it clear in multiple places that it's not okay for Christians to have same-sex sexual relationships. For example, in Paul's letter to the Romans, he presents gay and lesbian relationships as a consequence of people turning away from God (Romans 1:18–31), and in his first letter to the Corinthians, he lists gay relationships alongside cheating on your husband or wife, practicing other forms of sexual immorality, worshiping idols, stealing, constantly getting drunk, abusing people with your words, and other forms of sin as things that make us "unrighteous" and unable to "inherit the kingdom of God" (1 Corinthians 6:9–10). But Paul is not saying all of this to keep people *out* of God's kingdom but to invite them in! He points out that some of the Corinthian Christians had done *all* of these things. Then he says, "But you were washed, you were sanctified, you were justified in the name of the Lord Jesus Christ and by the Spirit of our God" (1 Corinthians 6:11).

When Rachel discovered that the Bible really was against gay relationships, she was very upset. She thought she might want to start following Jesus. But she didn't want to give up her dream of marrying a woman. In the end, though, she decided Jesus was demanding her total allegiance: following him meant being willing to give up *anything* else, and life with Jesus was worth it. In fact, if Jesus really had the power to make her right with God and to welcome her into eternal life, it would be stupid to say no to him for the sake of any human love. But for a long time, while Rachel knew that the Bible said no to same-sex marriage, she didn't understand the reasons why. That's how many people feel today.

Love, Not Hate

For many people today, the Bible's no to same-sex marriage is a big reason for thinking Christianity isn't true. Many of my friends would say that the Bible only teaches that sex between two men or two women isn't okay because the people who wrote the Bible were hateful, self-righteous, and ignorant: they just didn't understand how two men or two women could have the kind of faithful, sexual love that goes with marriage. I can see why people think this. Sadly, many Christians have treated gay and lesbian people hatefully and looked down on them with self-righteous judgment. But that's not what the Bible calls us to.

Paul—who wrote many of the Bible passages that say gay relationships are not allowed for Christians—was intentionally single, so you might think he was being judgmental. But if we look more carefully, we find that Paul did not look down on people in gay relationships, as if he was better than they were. In fact, right after telling his friend Timothy that all sex outside marriage (including gay relationships) goes against God's plan (1 Timothy 1:8–11), Paul said that he himself was the *worst* sinner and that Jesus saved him to show that even someone as terrible as Paul could be made right with God (1 Timothy 1:15–16)!

It's also not true that people in Jesus's day just didn't understand same-sex attraction. Like my friend Rachel, some of the first Christians had a history of gay relationships (1 Corinthians 6:9–11). They lived in a culture where many people thought it was okay for men (at least) to sleep with other men, as well as with women they weren't married to. While same-sex marriage wasn't generally practiced in the Roman empire, the notorious Emperor Nero, who ruled during the time when much of the New Testament was being written, at one point got dressed up as a woman and married another man.[5] The Christian insistence that sex only belonged in marriage between one man and one woman would have seemed as strange to many people back then as it does to people now. But as we have seen, the Bible says that sex and marriage isn't just about two people making each other happy. It's meant to be a little model of Jesus's love for his church.

If you've ever built a model airplane, you know that the pieces (wings, cockpit, tail, wheels, etc.) match up with pieces of a real airplane. Likewise, the pieces of Christian marriage match up with Jesus's love for his church. Jesus's love is faithful and forever, so marriage must be to just one person until death. Jesus's love is life-giving and creative. So marriage is the place to create new humans. Jesus's love is sacrificial, so husbands are called to sacrifice for their wives. And Jesus is different from us, so marriage is a love across difference: male and female. In fact, God designed humans so that the differences between a man's body and a woman's body would be the exact thing that enables men and women to have babies together. Switching the design of marriage to two men or two women is like putting two left wings on your model plane: it doesn't match the original.

Of course—just as a model plane doesn't *really* fly—marriage isn't half as good as Jesus's love. That's why it's totally fine *not* to get married. In fact, the Bible says that staying single can actually be better than getting married (1 Corinthians 7:7, 32–35). Jesus wasn't married. Paul wasn't married. If we're following Jesus, we don't need another sinful human to "complete" us. Some of the most wonderful Christians I know are single. For example, my friend Lou (whom I mentioned earlier) serves our church community in a hundred different, valuable ways: from making meals for homeless people to leading singing at our church summer camp. Or my friend Mary is a single woman and one of the best Bible teachers I know. Single people of all ages play vital roles in the church and help us all to see that relationship with Jesus is the most important thing. Likewise, good marriages help us all understand a bit more of what the Bible means when it says that Jesus loves us. But marriage isn't the only relationship that points us to Jesus's love. In fact, far from being *against* same-sex love, the Bible calls us to love people of our own sex very deeply!

Greater Love Has No One Than This

As we saw earlier, we glimpse God's love for us through the love of the best fathers and mothers for their kids, and in the love of the best husbands for their wives. But we also find echoes of God's love in friendship.

Maybe you know how special friendship closeness is. Or maybe you long for close friends and haven't found them yet. If we believe what Jesus says, friendship is very precious. In fact, it's one of the very *best* windows into his love: "Greater love has no one than this," said Jesus, "that someone lay down his life for his friends" (John 15:13).

The Bible says that Christians are "one body" together (Romans 12:5), that we are brothers and sisters (Matthew 12:50), "knit together in love" (Colossians 2:2), and comrades in arms (Philippians 2:25). Paul calls his friend Onesimus his "very heart" (Philemon 12), and he says he was among the Christians in Thessalonica like "a nursing mother taking care of her own children" (1 Thessalonians 2:7). This is very intimate language. But it is not sexual.

People will sometimes ask, "Are you in a relationship?" when they mean, "Do you have a boyfriend or girlfriend?" But in the Bible, friendship is a very important relationship. Unlike marriage, it's a kind of relationship that we can enjoy with lots of different people all at once. In fact, God made us to have multiple friends! And while we can certainly enjoy friendship with someone of the opposite sex, the deepest friendship intimacy is a particular gift for people of the same sex.

A few months ago, a woman whose partner is also a woman said she felt sorry for me because I had "never experienced love or passion with another woman." I told my friend Rachel about this and Rachel replied, "She's wrong about the love!" Like Rachel, I've said no to romantic relationships with other women. But I enjoy deep, joyful, God-given love with my close female friends—like my friend Natasha, who has been my best friend since we were both sixteen, and whom I text with every day, even though we live on different continents! But that doesn't mean it's always easy to say no to our desires.

Saying No to Our Desires Is Hard

Not long after Rachel started following Jesus, her ex-girlfriend called her and wanted to make up. Rachel managed to say no that day. But she ended up having a sexual relationship with another young woman at Yale, and even went back to her ex-girlfriend for a time when she thought she'd been a Christian long enough to resist that attraction. Gradually, with the help of God's Spirit and the love of Christian friends, Rachel was able to grow in her obedience and learn to say no to her desires. But it wasn't easy.

The fact is that all of us will likely sometimes be attracted to people we're not married to. This is true whether you're attracted to the same sex or the opposite sex, and it's true whether you're single or married. If we're followers of Jesus, we'll need help when those feelings arise. We'll also need assurance of God's forgiveness if—like Rachel as a young believer in college—we fail big-time. That's where Jesus comes in.

Jesus wasn't soft on sexual sin. The Old Testament taught that it was wrong to commit adultery by sleeping with someone you're not married to. But Jesus said if you even look at a woman lustfully you have already committed adultery in your heart (Matthew 5:27–28). That means that pretty much *all of us* who are old enough to have sexual desires have sinned, because we've all looked lustfully at people we're not married to. But Jesus also taught that *none of us* are beyond his love and forgiveness. In fact, Jesus was often criticized for spending time with people others thought of as sexual sinners, and he spends time with sexual sinners today, offering love, forgiveness, and help.

For some followers of Jesus, a big area where they need forgiveness and help is with looking at sexual images on screens.

Looking through Screens instead of Windows

Real relationships take risk. We risk our hearts when we reach out to someone else. Because of this, looking at pornography (sexual videos or photos) can seem like a safer route. Maybe that's a path you've chosen, or maybe you discovered sexual images by accident on a phone or computer screen, those images got stuck in your head, and you've found yourself going back for more. If that's you, you're not alone. By the age of fifteen, as many as one in three people have looked at pornography online, and it can affect both boys and girls.

Watching pornography might feel good in the moment, but—like any other drug—it can leave us feeling empty and make it harder for us to relate to others.[6] Pornography also hurts the people we are watching. Their bodies are being used in ways that undermine their value. Plugging into imaginary people unplugs us from real people—or worse, it makes us treat real people as if they're imaginary: just there to fulfill our fantasies.

Maybe you've acted like that. Or maybe that's how other people have treated you. Either way, a phone or a computer screen is not a window into real love. It's a fake to break our hearts. Slowly. Click by click. Like a hammer, chipping away at a stone. You're worth more than that. So are the people you're watching.

If you find yourself stuck looking at sexual photos or videos, get help and break free.[7] Like many other forms of sin, pornography makes us ashamed to ask for help from friends or mentors, because we think they won't understand. But you don't need to be ashamed. Many people have this struggle, and Jesus is ready to forgive you as soon as you ask. One time, when religious people were criticizing Jesus for hanging out with "sinners" he told them that it wasn't the healthy who needed a doctor but the sick (Luke 5:31). What the religious people didn't realize was that they were just as sick as the "sinners" they despised. But because they thought they were good, they weren't coming to Jesus.

We All Need Help

Growing up, I knew the Bible was against same-sex romance, but I didn't know that it was okay to talk about my feelings of attraction to other girls. So I just kept quiet and hoped and prayed my feelings would go away. If you can relate to that, I'd encourage you to talk to one or two trusted Christian friends. If you *can't* relate, think about how you could be a trusted friend for someone else, whether they're struggling with same-sex attraction, pornography addiction, or resisting a sexual relationship with a boyfriend or girlfriend. Jesus doesn't want Christians to bear things alone. He gives us brothers and sisters in Christ to help us along the way. I wish now that I'd talked to Christian friends growing up instead of hiding my feelings and hoping they'd disappear.

When my attractions didn't change, I had to trust that Jesus's love was better than the love any woman could give me. I still have to trust that today. Despite being married to a wonderful man, I have to trust Jesus with the piece of me that sometimes longs for romance with a woman. If you're a follower of Jesus, you'll have to trust your unfulfilled desires to Jesus too—whomever you're attracted to, and whether you get married or not. All of us have to say no to some of our longings in order to say yes to Jesus. And we all need each other for help along the way.

We All Need Love

God made us to thrive with multiple close relationships: with brothers and sisters, parents, friends, and—for some of us— husbands, wives, and kids. Like a spider weaving its web, we need multiple points of connection to thrive. We're not designed to dangle from a single thread! At the heart of the web is Jesus: the One who made us and who loves us more than anyone else ever could. He is the only person who can make all our dreams of love come true.

In the made-up story of *Frozen*, Anna showed her love for Elsa by being willing to die to save her sister. In the true story of Jesus, we see that same kind of love. "By this we know love," said Jesus's friend John, "that he laid down his life for us" (1 John 3:16). Anna's act of true love saved her sister's life and thawed her own frozen heart. Jesus's act of true love paid for our sin and won us eternal life with him in the closest relationship we could ever imagine—closer than marriage, closer than friendship, as close as a head with a body. Put your trust in Jesus and nothing—not even death itself—will be able to separate you from that love (Romans 8:35–39).

- Our culture says that "Love is love," so it's fine for someone to have a romantic and sexual relationship with someone of their same sex. The Bible says that "God is love," and that he gives us glimpses of his love through different kinds of relationship: including parent to child, husband to wife, and friend to friend.

- In the Bible, human marriage is a picture of Jesus's relationship with his people. This is a faithful, exclusive, life-creating, never-ending love, and it is a love across difference. So human marriage is designed to be faithful, exclusive, life-creating, never-ending, and across the difference of male and female.

- No human marriage will ever be as good as Jesus's relationship with us. Marriage at its best is just a little scale model of a much greater reality.

- Singleness isn't second best. The Bible says being single (like Paul) can be even better than being married.

- Sex is a good gift in marriage, but it does not belong in other relationships. In particular, it does not belong in relationships between adults and kids. If you are experiencing sexual touching from an adult, tell someone you trust and get help.

- The Bible is clear that same-sex sexual relationships are not okay for Christians. But instead of being judgmental and hateful of people in gay relationships, Christians are called to love their gay and lesbian friends and to share the gospel with them just as they would with any other nonbelievers.

- All Christians will need to say no to romantic desire and sexual attraction at times. This is often hard, and we need help from God's Spirit and from his people. We're not meant to struggle alone.

- Like illegal drugs, pornography is addictive and destructive, and it ultimately leaves us feeling miserable and alone. If you're stuck in a pornography addiction, turn to Jesus for forgiveness and get help from friends and mentors to break free.
- Friendship is one of the greatest pictures of Jesus's love for us. God has designed us to enjoy multiple close friendships and to find help and encouragement through them.
- Jesus's love is the greatest love there is. It's worth giving up any other relationship for him.

Who Cares If You're a Boy or a Girl?

É owyn in *The Lord of the Rings* is my all-time favorite heroine. When her uncle, King Théoden, rides out with his men to fight against the Dark Lord, Sauron, Éowyn desperately wants to go too. But she's a woman, so she is told she must stay behind. Sauron's armies are led by the Witch-king of Angmar—an undead power so terrifying that all the men flee before him. King Théoden gets thrown off his horse and is about to be killed. But one knight stands to protect the fallen king.

The Witch-king laughs and recites a prophesy about himself: "Thou fool! No living man may hinder me!"[1] But the knight laughs back. She takes off her helmet, her hair streams down, and she retorts,

But no living man am I! You look upon a woman. Éowyn I am. Éomund's daughter. You stand between me and my lord and kin. Begone, if you be not deathless! For living or dark undead, I will smite you, if you touch him.[2]

The scene is breathtaking. Éowyn's love-fueled courage draws me like a magnet. She's the kind of woman I want to be.

In this chapter, we're going to ask some important questions. What does the Bible say about men and women? Is Christianity good or bad for women? Does following Jesus mean you have to fit in with everything people expect of boys and girls? Should Christians be free to identify as the opposite sex, or with neither sex, if our bodies don't match how we feel inside? What does the Bible say about people who are born "intersex"—with bodies that are not typically male *or* female?

These questions make us wonder, "What does it mean to be a man or a woman?" "Who am I really?" If Christianity is true, then the author of our lives is also the author of the Bible. And if we want to understand our own story, we need to understand God's big story.

So we'll start at the beginning.

In the Beginning

According to many ancient philosophies, men were more important than women. But the Bible tells a different story. God made humans—"male and female"—"in his own image" (Genesis 1:26–28). Men and women are equally important. But they are also importantly different.

When you think about it, God could have designed things so that you didn't need both a man and a woman to make a baby. He could have miraculously made a new crop of people every twenty years or so, or he could have made us like amoebas, that can reproduce by themselves. But instead, God made us male *and* female and designed us so that new humans could be created via the deep connection between a man and a woman that pictures Jesus's love for his church.

In Genesis 2, God makes the man first and then says, "It is not good that the man should be alone," so he makes the woman as a "helper" (Genesis 2:18). This might sound like the woman is less important: just a "helper." But in the Bible, the word "helper" usually describes God himself (e.g., Psalm 54:4; 118:7), so it *can't* mean women are less important than men! Instead, we see that men and women are meant to do God's work together.

So what does the Bible say about what it means to be a man or a woman?

The Perfect Man

The Bible gives us a picture of the one and only perfect man. Jesus is the perfect "image of the invisible God" (Colossians 1:15). He had the power to stop storms (Mark 4:35–41), summon angels (Matthew 26:53), and defeat death (John 11:25). But his arms held little children (Mark 10:13–16), and his hands reached out to heal the sick (Matthew 8:3; Luke 4:40). Jesus drove money-changers out of God's temple with a whip (John 2:13–17). But he tenderly welcomed the lonely, rejected, and weak (Matthew 11:28–30). When his friend Lazarus died, Jesus wept (John 11:35). When his friend Peter drew his sword to protect Jesus from getting arrested, Jesus healed the man Peter had hurt (Luke 22:49–51). Jesus is the greatest hero in the history of the world. But he fought his greatest battle by dying on a cross. Jesus is the rightful King of all the world, but he came "not to be served but to serve" (Mark 10:45). Before his crucifixion, Jesus washed his disciples' feet (John 13), and after his resurrection, he cooked them breakfast (John 21:9).

Some people think *real* men don't cry. But Jesus cried. Some people think *real* men sleep with lots of women. But Jesus never even had a girlfriend. Some people think *real* men don't stand for insults. But Jesus took insults all day long. He defended the weak, but he wouldn't fight back to defend himself. Some people think real men don't cook or care for kids. But Jesus did both these things. If we want to know what it means to be a perfect man, we must look at Jesus.

Women are called to copy Jesus too. He is the perfect human, so all Christians—male or female—are called to imitate him. But the ways in which Jesus used his strength and power for others, not himself, is a particular model for men, who often have more physical strength and have traditionally had more power (Philippians 2:1–11).

So what does the Bible say about women?

The Greatest Movement of Women in History!

Some of my friends think Christianity has pushed women down. But Christianity actually lifted women up. We may take it for granted that women are equally valuable as men. But that was not what people in Jesus's day believed.

As we saw in chapter 4, when Jesus was born, it was normal for people to leave baby girls outside to die. They thought girls were less important than boys. But Jesus's teachings changed that. Jesus made lots of female friends and treated them as if they were equal to men. For instance, when his friend Mary was sitting at his feet to learn alongside his male disciples, Jesus defended her (Luke 10:38–42). He particularly cared for women other people looked down on. Jesus shocked his disciples by befriending a Samaritan woman, who had had five husbands and was now living with a man she wasn't married to (John 4:1–42), and he held up a "sinful woman" who loved him as a moral example to a self-righteous man who didn't (Luke 7:36–50). As we saw in chapter 5, the first people to see Jesus after his resurrection were women—even though women at the time weren't trusted as witnesses in court!

Some of my friends think that Christianity is "misogynistic"—which means hateful toward women. Just like with any other sin, Christians have sometimes acted that way. But from the very beginning, Jesus has especially drawn women to himself. Historians believe that in the Greco-Roman empire into which Jesus was born, there may have been twice as many men as women, because women often died in childbirth and baby girls were often left outside to die.[3] But the church seems to have been the other way around, with perhaps twice as many women as men.[4] The second-century Greek philosopher Celsus mocked Christians saying that they "are able to convince only the foolish, dishonorable and stupid, only slaves, women, and little children."[5] Today, both in America and across the world, there are significantly more Christian women than men, and women are more likely to go to church, read the Bible, and pray.[6] Christianity isn't *against* women: it's the greatest movement of women in all of history!

What about Feminism?

Some people think that Christianity is against *feminism*, which is defined as, "the advocacy of women's rights on the basis of the equality of the sexes." But as we have seen, Christianity was actually the reason people started to think that women are equal to men. In fact, many of the first modern feminists were Christians.

Women like Sojourner Truth (whom we met in chapter 2) and Lucretia Mott campaigned both for women's rights and for the rights of black people, recognizing that God made *all* humans in his image. Early Christian feminists argued that women were equal to men and so they should have the same rights as men to do things like vote in elections, own houses, work jobs, and be paid fairly for their work. They believed women were equal to men not *in spite of* their faith in Jesus but *because* of it!

In the Bible, we see the work of women valued in all sorts of ways. From a Christian perspective, work is valuable whether it is paid or unpaid, and caring for children is extremely important work. Some of my most intelligent and talented Christian friends feel called to care for their kids full time. But raising kids is not the only job women are called to do. When Paul lists his ministry partners at the end of his letter to the Romans, he names nine women, including Phoebe who delivered the letter (Romans 16:1) and two sisters (we think) named Tryphaena and Tryphosa, whom he calls "workers in the Lord" (Romans 16:12). We don't know whether these women had children or not, but we do know that they were doing the vital work of spreading the good news about Jesus.

We also know that some of the first female Christians had paid jobs outside the home. For example, Lydia is one of the people whose conversion story we read about in the book of Acts. We don't know whether or not she had children, but we do know that she had a household and that she was a founding member of the church in Philippi. Lydia is described as a "seller of purple goods" (Acts 16:14). We also know that Jesus himself was supported by money from some of his female followers (Luke 8:2–3), so there is no reason to think that Christian women should not work outside the home and be paid fairly for their work.

For these reasons, I would be comfortable saying I'm a feminist: I'm happy to argue for women to have rights equal to men. I'm thankful for the opportunity to be both a mother and someone who is paid for working outside the home. I believe that women should have the right to vote, and that they should be paid equally to men for doing the same work. But many Christians would not want to identify as feminists—despite believing that men and women are equal in God's sight—because some of the beliefs that get mixed in with feminism today are things that Christians can't accept. The most important example is a practice known as abortion, which we discussed in chapter 4.

From the beginnings of the church, Christians have stood against surrounding cultures to say that babies are precious human beings in their own right and not property. Throughout history, the vast majority of babies who have died by abortion (before birth) or infanticide (after birth) have been girls. This is still true globally today. The idea that being "pro-choice" (in favor of abortion) means being pro-women does not fit with this reality.

I also don't think a society that promotes sex without commitment—which often results in unplanned pregnancies that can end in abortion—is pro-women. As we saw in chapter 7, sex without commitment tends to be *bad* for women's happiness. In America, over 80 percent of women who have abortions are not married and can't count on the support of the baby's father.[7] Arguing for abortion is known as being "pro-choice." But many women feel like they *don't* have a choice, even if they want to keep the baby, because they don't have enough support.

Many of the changes brought about by feminism in the last hundred years have been positive. Women have gained voting rights, more opportunities, and greater equality. But building a society in which commitment-free sex is promoted, the unique ability of women to carry and give birth to children is not highly valued, and pregnant women are often not properly supported does not strike me as pro-women: in fact, quite the opposite.

So Does It Matter If We're Male or Female?

As we saw in chapter 2, in Jesus's family, everyone is equal. Paul wrote to some of the first Christians, "There is neither Jew nor Greek, there is neither slave nor free, there is no male and female, for you are all one in Christ Jesus" (Galatians 3:28). Whatever our race, or situation, or sex, we are all equally precious to God. But God made us male and female on purpose, and in some parts of life—for example, in marriage, as we saw in chapter 7—he calls men and women to different roles.

I played soccer in college, and my job was to manage the defense. Everyone on our team had one aim: to make sure we got more goals than the other team. But we had different roles. The strikers weren't more important than the goalie. They simply had a different job. In the team of God's people, everyone has the same aim: worshiping God, loving others, and telling people about Jesus. But we all have different roles on the team. In some areas, these roles depend on whether God made us male or female.

Throughout the last two thousand years, women have played a massive role in spreading the message of Jesus. Both men and women are called to this work. But a few Christians in each church are called to teach the Bible to the whole church and lead God's family in that place. These people are often called pastors and elders, and these roles seem to be given in the Bible to qualified men. Paul connects this back to the story of Adam and Eve, where Adam was created first and given the commandment not to eat the fruit of the tree of the knowledge of good and evil before Eve was created (1 Timothy 2:11–14; Genesis 2:15–3:7). Adam was trusted with that message. But then Satan (posing as a serpent) came and lied to Eve and questioned God's command. He told her that if she ate fruit from that tree she would become like God. Eve ate the fruit, and instead of stopping Eve, Adam chose to eat the fruit as well. In this story, there were only two humans living under God's rule. But Paul's point seems to be that Adam should have been the one to answer the serpent as he was given the commandment by God in the first place, and that God has given men a particular responsibility to teach and lead in the church.

This is not because women aren't as intelligent or as faithful as men, or because a woman couldn't be as good a speaker or leader as a man. As we have seen, the first people to see Jesus after he was raised from the dead were women, and it seems like the women believed that Jesus had been raised, while the male disciples still doubted (e.g., Luke 24:10–11). Paul also highlights many women as his fellow workers in the gospel (e.g., Romans 16:1–16; Philippians 4:2–3).

The fact that men are called to lead local churches also doesn't mean that men are more important than women. When two of Jesus's disciples, James and John, asked to have special leadership positions in his kingdom, Jesus explained to them that leadership in his kingdom was the *opposite* of leadership in the world. In the world, people take charge so they can get their own way. But Jesus explained that in his kingdom, "whoever would be great among you must be your servant, and whoever would be first among you must be slave of all. For even the Son of Man [that's Jesus] came not to be served but to serve, and to give his life as a ransom for many" (Mark 10:43–45). Leaders in Jesus's kingdom don't come first. They come last.

At the time when the New Testament was being written (and in many parts of the world today) teaching the Bible in public often meant getting attacked or arrested. So perhaps it's not surprising that God calls men to sacrifice in marriage and to lead in church. It's not about power and privilege. It's about his special call on men to serve and sacrifice, like Jesus served and sacrificed for us.

So God made men and women equal, but in some areas he has called them to different roles. But what about people who are born with bodies that are neither fully male nor fully female?

What about People Born Intersex?

A few years ago, a good friend of mine had a baby who was born intersex. The baby looked physically more like a girl. But when the doctors checked, they found the baby didn't have a uterus (the organ designed to carry a developing, new baby) but did have testes (the organs that produce sperm). My friends are raising their child as a girl. Right now, this child seems comfortable as a girl. In fact, she seems to like all the things that our culture usually associates with little girls. But we don't know how she will feel when she grows up, and her parents are ready to give her lots of space to work through that as she gets older.

In Jesus's day, some people were also born intersex. Other people were born male, but had their testes removed so they could do particular jobs—like sing with a high voice or protect a king's wives. This is a horrible thing to do to a child, but sadly it was quite common in the ancient world. People who had had this done to them were called *eunuchs*. One of Jesus's first followers was a eunuch (Acts 8:26–40), and Jesus talked about eunuchs, right after he taught that marriage was between one man and one woman for life (Matthew 19:3–12). Jesus valued marriage. But he also valued singleness and taught that people who don't get married or aren't able to have children are very valuable in his kingdom too. So the fact that intersex people are often unable to have children doesn't make them any less precious in Jesus's sight or any less useful in Jesus's mission. Jesus himself never had kids, and he is the perfect human!

So how does being intersex relate to being transgender?

What about People Who Identify as Transgender?

Some people argue that because babies are occasionally born intersex, "male" and "female" are not clear categories, but that everyone is on a spectrum with completely male at one end and completely female at the other. They also say that our bodies don't have to define whether we are a man or a woman, but that if someone's feelings don't match their body, they should be able to decide whether they want to be recognized as male or female—or perhaps as "non-binary" or "gender non-conforming," meaning they don't want to be recognized as either a man or a woman.

Someone who was born with a male body but later identifies as a woman would be described today as a *trans* or *transgender woman* and someone who was born with a female body but identifies as a man would be described as a *trans* or *transgender man.* Transgender people often take new names. For example, someone called John might switch to Jane and ask people to use "she" or "her" instead of "he" or "him." Someone who identifies as non-binary or gender non-conforming might ask to be talked about as "they." So what does Christianity say about all of this?

To begin with, it's important for us to listen to other people and understand their feelings and experiences. When I was a kid, I didn't want to wear dresses and play with dolls. I wanted to sword fight with my brother in the woods. My mum made me do ballet. I hated it. Someone once gave me a pink "My Little Pony" for my birthday. I flushed it down the toilet. (Don't try this: it's really bad for the toilet!) I don't recall wanting to *be* a boy. That was never an option in my mind. But at my all-girls school, I acted every male role I could. As a teenager, I never wanted to paint my nails, wear makeup, shop for clothes, or talk about boys. Girly things weren't my thing.

Some teens feel like I did, except much, much more. They feel like the body they were born with doesn't match how they feel on the inside. Some people choose to dress in ways typical of the opposite sex. They might also take medicines or have surgeries to make their bodies look like the opposite sex. If you have never felt this way, it can be hard to understand why someone would do this. Sadly, people who feel this way have often been laughed at or bullied. It is never right for Christians to mock and bully people. Jesus calls us to love others—especially if they are different from us. But Christians also believe that God made us male and female on purpose. So how should Christians think about someone wanting to change their gender identity?

First, we know that Jesus cares a lot about our feelings. He knows us from the inside out. He knows what we love and what makes us scared or sad. He knows when we feel like we don't fit in and when we wish we could be different. He loves us so much that he died for us! So if you are a boy, but you desperately wish you were a girl, or if you are a girl who longs to be a boy, Jesus sees you and knows you and loves you with an everlasting love.

Second, the Bible tells us that God created everything *through* Jesus (John 1:3). Jesus made you. If you were born a boy, he meant for you to be a boy. If you were born a girl, he meant for you to be a girl. This doesn't mean that it will always be easy, or that you have to do everything other people expect from girls or boys. As we saw earlier, Jesus cried, and cooked, and loved babies, and when people beat him up, he didn't fight back. If you're a follower of Jesus, it's okay to be different. Unlike lots of women, I hate fashion and shopping for clothes. But my husband, Bryan, likes both those things—and that's okay! But the Bible also teaches us that we shouldn't always trust our feelings. We find our true selves not by following our feelings, but by following Jesus, so when our desires don't line up with following Jesus, we need to trust him.

I shared in the last chapter that I tend to be romantically attracted to women. But being a Christian means learning to trust Jesus more than my feelings and saying no to romantic relationships with women. If I felt a deep desire to be a man and not a woman, I would need to trust Jesus with that desire too. In fact, following Jesus *always* means trusting him with our desires, even if it's really hard. Jesus said, "If anyone would come after me, let him deny himself and take up his cross and follow me. For whoever would save his life will lose it, but whoever loses his life for my sake will find it" (Matthew 16:24–25). But Jesus doesn't ask us to do this alone. He gives us his Spirit, and he gives us his body (other Christians) for help. So if you are struggling with being a boy or a girl, look for a Christian friend to talk to about your feelings. If you feel comfortable with your body, try to be the kind of person who could support a friend who is struggling in this way.

How Should Christians Relate to Transgender People?

If you're a Christian and some of your classmates identify as transgender or non-binary, your job is not to avoid them or make fun of them. Your job is to tell them about Jesus and show them his love—just as you would to others. Loving people doesn't mean agreeing with all their decisions. My non-Christian friends make all sorts of decisions I disagree with. They're not working from the same roadmap. But I can still love them and listen to them. In fact, listening to someone's story is often the best starting point for showing love. Everyone wants to be known and understood. At times, though, loving someone means telling them when you don't think they're making the right decision.

In one of my favorite moments in the Harry Potter series, Neville helps Gryffindor win the House Cup, because he stood up to Harry, Ron, and Hermione when he thought they were doing the wrong thing. Dumbledore gives Neville five points for this act of courage saying, "It takes a great deal of bravery to stand up to our enemies, but just as much to stand up to our friends."[8] Questioning whether it's the right decision for someone to live as the opposite sex, perhaps even taking medications or having surgeries to change their bodies in ways they can never reverse, can be seen as being hateful in our culture today. But telling a friend that you love them as they are, and that you think the body they were born with is good isn't hateful. All of us make decisions in light of what our friends and family think and sometimes we need encouragement from our friends to accept ourselves.

It can be easy to think that making a change to our bodies is the key to happiness—whether it's getting thinner, or stronger, or taller, or having larger breasts, or changing whether we are seen as a boy or as a girl. But just as it's not hateful to tell a friend you love her at just the weight she is, it's not hateful to tell a friend you love her as a girl, or that you love him as a boy, even if our friends don't fit the stereotypes about boys and girls that say, "Girls should be like this and boys should be like that." What's more, when you think about it, if we no longer let our bodies tell us if we are male or female, those stereotypes are all we have left. Let me explain.

What Do "Man" and "Woman" Mean?

Earlier this year, the actor (Daniel Radcliffe) who played Harry Potter in the films of J. K. Rowling's books made a public statement: "Transgender women are women." When he said this, he meant that people who were born with a male body but feel like they belong in the world as a woman should be recognized as women just as much as people who were born with a female body. Daniel Radcliffe said this in response to J. K. Rowling herself saying that—while she personally thinks it's okay for people to live in the world as the opposite sex—the bodies we are born with and grew up with still matter, and that someone who was born male should not be treated as female in every situation. Some people were very angry with J. K. Rowling for saying this, and Daniel

Radcliffe wanted to make clear that he didn't agree. But Daniel Radcliffe's statement highlights an important question: What does "man" or "woman" mean?

Up until recently in our culture, for me to say, "I am a woman" would mean—first and foremost—that I was born with a female body. There are significant differences between male bodies and female bodies. Even beyond what we can see with our eyes, scientists could tell whether you were a boy or a girl by examining a single cell from anywhere in your body.[9] But if Daniel Radcliffe's claim that "transwomen are women" is true, and being born with a female body *isn't* at the heart of what it means to be a woman, then what *does* it mean to be a woman? Does it mean wearing dresses and makeup, or wearing your hair long rather than short? Some women in our culture do those things, but no one would say that was the definition of being a woman. Does it mean other people *thinking* you were born with a female body? If so, then the identity of a transgender person would depend on people not knowing the truth about his or her past.

In conversations about transgender questions, people often talk as if there is something deep inside of us—not connected with our bodies—that defines whether we are male or female more than our bodies do. But while some people struggle with their gender identity throughout their life, others who feel uncomfortable with their bodies as teenagers find that those feelings change as they get older.[10] If there was something other than our bodies that more truly defined us as male or female, we would expect that sense of identity always to stay the same throughout someone's life. Many people today think that Christians are foolish for believing things that cannot be measured with the tools of science. But the idea that there is a thing deep within us that tells us if we are male or female against the evidence of our physical bodies does not line up with science at all. And we are still left with the question: What does it mean to be a man or a woman, if it doesn't relate to our biological sex?

As a Christian, I am not surprised that our society is struggling to define what it means to be a man or a woman. As we saw in chapter 6, without belief in a Creator God who made humans in his image, we are left without a real definition of what it means to be a human being, so no wonder we don't know what it means to be a male or female human. As we saw in chapter 4, without belief in a Creator God who gives us moral laws, we are like cartoon characters who have run off a cliff and keep running in midair for a few seconds before we crash to the ground.

As a Christian, I do believe that there is a voice deep inside me that tells me who I am. That voice is God's Spirit, who unites every believer to Jesus like a body to its head, or a wife to her husband. The Spirit speaks through God's word (the Bible) and guides his people. But from a Christian perspective, this voice inside isn't disconnected from our bodies, because the same God who lives within us by his Spirit also *created* our bodies. Jesus tells us that God created humans "from the beginning male and female" (Matthew 19:4). If we're trusting in Jesus, he knows us from the inside out, and he makes us belong even when we feel like we don't fit. Growing up, I often felt inadequate as a woman. I still sometimes feel that way today. But when I do, I trust Jesus that he made me a woman on purpose and that he loves me just as I am.

What's Your Story?

Éowyn didn't fit in with other women, and yet because she was a woman, she was left behind when her uncle rode to war. But J. R. R. Tolkien, who wrote *The Lord of the Rings*, gave Éowyn the special role of defeating the Witch-king of Angmar—and it was a job she could do only *because* she was a woman! Tolkien was an incredible storyteller. But God is even better. And if you're a follower of Jesus, he is the author of your story. He made you the boy or girl that you are, even if you don't feel like you fit. I don't know what he's planning, or how he's going to use you on his team. But I do know this: God has promised that in all things he is working for the good of those who love him (Romans 8:28) and that if we lose the things we want for Jesus's sake, we will end up finding them in an even better way. You can count on that. Now. And forever.

- God made both men and women in his image. We are equally valuable and useful to his mission.
- Jesus is the perfect man. He always used his strength to serve others, and he did many things that don't fit with male stereotypes.
- Jesus's teachings and actions changed how women were viewed in society.
- Christianity is not against women. There have always been more Christian women than men. In fact, Christianity is the greatest movement of and for women in all of history.
- There are many things to which both men and women are called, but the Bible gives men and women different roles to play in marriage and certain roles in the church seem to be given to men. This doesn't make men more important. In Jesus's kingdom, leadership is about service and sacrifice, not power and privilege.
- Some people are born "intersex"—with bodies that are neither fully male nor fully female. Intersex people are precious to God and useful in Jesus's mission.
- Some people struggle with their gender identity and want to be recognized as the opposite sex from the bodies they were born with—or as being neither sex. But the Bible tells us that God made us male and female on purpose and that we should trust him more than we trust our feelings, even when that is really hard.
- Christians are called to love and befriend transgender folk, just as they are called to love all people. This means Christians should listen to people who identify as transgender or non-binary and try to understand their stories and feelings. But it doesn't mean Christians must affirm a friend's decision to live as the opposite

sex. Loving people doesn't mean agreeing with all their decisions. Sometimes it means challenging them.

- If the idea of being a man or a woman is separated out from having a male or a female body, we are left without any real idea of what being a man or a woman actually means. But if there is no God who created us in his image in the first place, we don't know what it means to be a human being either, so it's not surprising that we don't know what it means to be a man or a woman.

- Christians can trust that God made them male or female on purpose and that he will use them as a man or as a woman in his mission—even if we feel deeply uncomfortable with our sex. He is the author of our story, and we can trust him with our very lives.

Does God Care When We Hurt?

In *Harry Potter and the Deathly Hallows,* Harry comes to a sickening realization: Professor Dumbledore had planned for him to die. Dumbledore had given Harry the mission of destroying the seven "horcruxes" that held parts of Lord Voldemort's soul. What Harry didn't know was that he himself was one. But Dumbledore knew. "How neat, how elegant, not to waste any more lives," Harry reflects, "but to give the dangerous task to the boy who had already been marked for slaughter." Harry feels bitterly betrayed. "He had never questioned his own assumption that Dumbledore wanted him alive."[1]

As we look back over Harry's life, we see Dumbledore's role in Harry's suffering from the first. When Harry was orphaned as a baby, Dumbledore left him with his horrible aunt and uncle. Aunt Petunia had hated Harry's mother, and she hated Harry. "You had suffered," Dumbledore admits. "I knew you would when I left you on your aunt and uncle's doorstep. I knew I was condemning you to ten dark and difficult years."[2] Harry had been raised without love. He was routinely beaten up by his cousin, Dudley, who also made sure Harry didn't make friends at school. Even before Harry faced the epic suffering of death-defying conflict in the magical world, he faced the day-to-day suffering of a lonely, loveless, bullied childhood. Why? Because Dumbledore thought it was best.

Christians believe that the God who made the universe is in control of everything. In fact, the Bible claims that "for those who love God all things work together for good" (Romans 8:28). But how can we believe that? If there *is* a God in charge of everything —a God with even more power over us than Dumbledore had over Harry—why would he let bad things happen? How can we believe that God is full of power *and* love when he lets wars break out, families break up, kids get bullied, and babies die?

This is a question everyone should ask. It would take a set of books longer than the Harry Potter series to answer it properly. But in this chapter, we will look at one story about Jesus and what it tells us about suffering. From this story, we'll see that God really is in charge, and that he really does care.

When Jesus Doesn't Come

Mary and Martha were two of Jesus's best friends. They'd welcomed Jesus to their house and heard him teach (Luke 10:38–42). One day, their brother Lazarus got sick. Really sick. But Mary and Martha knew a miracle worker. Thousands of sick people had come to Jesus, and he'd healed them. So they sent Jesus a message: "Lord, he whom you love is ill" (John 11:3). You'd think that Jesus would come at once, right? But no. John writes, "Jesus loved Martha and her sister and Lazarus. So, when he heard that Lazarus was ill, he stayed two days longer in the place where he was" (John 11:5–6).

How weird is that? John doesn't say, "Jesus loved his friends, but he was super busy with other things, so he couldn't come right away." He doesn't say, "Jesus didn't love his friends, so he thought he'd make them wait." John says that *because* Jesus loved his friends, he didn't come. In fact, Jesus waited until Lazarus was dead. And then he came.

What do we learn from this? One thing we learn is that there are times when God intends for us to suffer, not because he doesn't love us but because he does. We may not understand it at the time, just as Harry didn't understand why Dumbledore had left him with the Dursleys. But we know that Jesus loved Mary and Martha and Lazarus, and *because* he loved them, he didn't come.

Maybe you've had suffering in your life, and you've prayed really hard for God to take it away. Perhaps someone at school bullies you, and you've prayed that he would stop. But he hasn't. Or perhaps your mother got really sick, and you prayed for her to get better. But she didn't. Or maybe you prayed and prayed that your parents would stop fighting, but instead they got divorced.

If God loves us and he is in charge, we might think he'd take sad things away when we ask. Sometimes he does. I've certainly had that experience. But sometimes he doesn't. And I've had that happen too. Just like when Mary and Martha called for Jesus and he didn't come.

But that's not the end of the story.

Jesus Comes

When Jesus finally comes, Lazarus has been dead and buried for four days. Martha goes out to meet him. "Lord," she says, "if you had been here, my brother would not have died. But even now I know that whatever you ask from God, God will give you" (John 11:21–22). Isn't her faith amazing? Martha believes Jesus can heal her brother even though he's been dead for days! So does Jesus rush to bring Lazarus back from the dead? No. Instead, they talk.

"Your brother will rise again," says Jesus (John 11:23). Many Jews at that time believed that God would raise his people to life again at the end of time, so Martha responds, "I know that he will rise again, in the resurrection on the last day" (John 11:24). And yet we can almost hear her thinking, *But what about now, Jesus? What about now? Why won't you help me now?*

The Bible promises that God will put everything right for his people in the end. When Jesus comes back as King, there will be no more death or mourning or crying or pain (Revelation 21:4). But sometimes that doesn't feel very comforting. Martha believes that her brother will come back to life at the end of time. But she wants him back *now*. She knows how powerful Jesus is. She *knows* he could raise Lazarus right away. But he doesn't. Instead, Jesus looks into this heartbroken woman's eyes and says these astonishing words:

> I am the resurrection and the life. Whoever believes in me, though he die, yet shall he live, and everyone who lives and believes in me shall never die. Do you believe this? (John 11:25–26)

Martha wants to have her brother back more than anything in the world. She's desperate. Jesus could make her deepest wish come true. But instead of giving Martha her wish, Jesus tells her that what she most needs is not Lazarus, but Jesus himself. He *is* the resurrection and the life.

Sometimes, if we're honest, we want a gift more than we want the giver. In the Harry Potter series, Harry's cousin, Dudley, is very spoiled. His parents are always giving him gifts, and when he doesn't get what he wants, he screams and complains. He doesn't really want his parents. He wants what they can give him. But Harry's parents died when he was a baby, and when he looks in the "Mirror of Erised" that shows you the thing you most want, he sees himself with them. Just being with his parents is his most desperate wish. He doesn't want their money or their stuff. He wants *them*. And when Jesus looks into Martha's eyes, he tells her the greatest truth that you and I could ever learn: What we need the most is not what Jesus can give us. It's Jesus himself. He *is* the resurrection and the life.

Sometimes, we think of prayer like a vending machine. We put a coin of prayer in the machine, press the number for the thing that we want, and expect it to drop into our hands. If God really loves us, surely he'll give us the things we desire! When we don't get what we asked for, we think the machine must be broken. But God is not a means to an end. He *is* the end. He's not a vending machine. He's a person. He's not just the greatest gift giver in the history of the world. He's the greatest gift. And he meets us most tenderly in our suffering.

Jesus Weeps

Martha answers Jesus's question with stunning faith: "Yes, Lord; I believe that you are the Christ, the Son of God, who is coming into the world" (John 11:27). But then she calls Mary, who falls at Jesus's feet, and repeats her sister's complaint: "Lord, if you had been here, my brother would not have died" (John 11:32).

Like Mary and Martha, we can cry out to God in our suffering. In fact, the book of Psalms in the Bible is full of suffering people crying out to God and asking why he isn't helping them. I've been in that place myself; maybe you have too. Crying on the floor, asking the Lord, "Why won't you help me now?" If you are a follower of Jesus, you'll find yourself in that place before long. Lying, like Mary, at Jesus's feet and wondering why he didn't answer your prayer. So how does Jesus react to Mary? And how does he react to us, when we cry out in our pain? Jesus asks where Lazarus's body has been laid. And then we read one of the shortest and most surprising verses in the Bible: "Jesus wept" (John 11:35).

Why is Jesus so upset? If he had come when Mary and Martha called, Lazarus would not have died, and no one would be crying now. When people saw Jesus weeping, some thought he must have loved Lazarus very much. But others asked, "Could not he who opened the eyes of the blind man also have kept this man from dying?" (John 11:36–37). The answer is, yes. Jesus *could* have stopped Lazarus from dying. He chose not to. But even so, he cried with his friends.

Jesus is no faraway God, watching us suffer from a distance. He is the God who steps into our suffering. The prophet Isaiah calls him "a man of sorrows" (Isaiah 53:3), and we see in the Gospels how Jesus hurts for hurting people. When my kids are hurt, they want their dad. He holds them in his strong arms and comforts them. Sometimes, to help them, he has to do something painful, like hold ice on a bruise or pour antiseptic on a cut. Sometimes my kids cry and fight, as we all do in our suffering. But their daddy holds them and comforts them with his love, even when he has to do a painful thing.

When we suffer, Jesus holds us. He holds us in our heartbreak. He holds us in our fear. He weeps with us when we weep. He knows the end of the story, when he will one day wipe every tear from our eyes (Revelation 21:4). But this does not stop him from holding us now in our pain. In fact, pain is a place of special close-ness with him. Perhaps you've noticed this in your own life. We can laugh with anyone. But we tend to cry only with those closest to us; and the bond is strongest when their suffering matches ours, because we know they *really* understand.

In Jesus, we find the one person who knows all our heartache and our pain. Jesus was abandoned by his closest friends, beaten by strangers, stripped, abused, and hung up on a cross to die. If you've ever been let down or teased or bullied or felt alone or got terribly sick, Jesus knows how you feel. There is no wound of ours he cannot touch. He knows the end of the story, when he will make a whole new better world. And yet he weeps with us when we weep.

But that's not the end of the story.

Jesus Saves

When Jesus comes to Lazarus's tomb, he is deeply upset again, and he commands that the gravestone be taken away. (In those days, people were often buried in caves, with a stone covering the entrance.) Martha warns him, "Lord, by this time there will be an odor, for he has been dead four days" (John 11:39). But Jesus insists. He prays. Then he shouts, "Lazarus, come out!" And the dead man gets up and walks out of his grave (John 11:43–44).

I often tell this story to my kids. Unlike children in most of human history, they don't know many people who have died. If you haven't been close to people who have died, it's easy to forget that you'll die one day yourself. But I want my kids to know that when death comes, Jesus will be with them. And one day, when their bodies have rotted and their lives have been forgotten, Jesus will call them out of their graves. The one who called stars into being will also call them back from death to life. Jesus isn't *just* loving. He's also powerful.

When Harry finally goes to his death, he carries with him a "resurrection stone." It's hidden in the golden snitch from his first Quidditch match—a seemingly small gift from Dumbledore. Dumbledore planned for Harry to suffer and to die. But he also planned for him to come back to life. The words, "I open at the close," were engraved on the snitch. Harry didn't know how his life would be saved, but Dumbledore did. And when the time came, it was.

If we're trusting in Jesus, we're holding a resurrection stone in our hands. Nothing can snatch it away from us, because nothing can snatch us away from Jesus, who *is* the resurrection and the life (John 10:28–29; 11:25–26). The only man who has ever beaten death beat death for us. And he has promised to give us life: not just for a few more years, but forever.

Is It Worth It?

Harry was so famous in the wizarding world that if he'd grown up there, he might have turned out like his awful cousin, Dudley, who thought the world revolved around him. So Dumbledore chose for Harry to suffer a painful childhood living with his aunt and uncle, not because he didn't care about Harry, but because he did. Dumbledore sent Harry to his death, clutching the resurrection stone, not because he wanted Harry dead, but because he wanted him finally to live life free of Voldemort.

The question we must ask when we see suffering is this: What could possibly be worth it? Jesus's flabbergasting claim is that he is. If you're trusting in Jesus, you can be sure that any suffering you face is not because he doesn't love you, but because he does. This doesn't mean we'll always understand. Often, we won't. The Bible is full of suffering people crying out to God and asking, "Why?" There are no easy answers. But if Jesus was willing to suffer and die for us, we can trust him even with our most terrible hurts. He is the resurrection and the life. He is writing our story right to the end. And if we're trusting in him, that ending will be unimaginably good (Romans 8:18).

- God is in control of all things, including our suffering.
- God doesn't let us suffer because he doesn't love us. He meets us in our suffering and promises to bring us through it.
- Jesus isn't a means to an end to change our circumstances. He is the end. He isn't just a way to get a better life. He is the resurrection and the life.
- The point of prayer isn't mostly to get things from Jesus, but to get Jesus himself.
- Even though Jesus knows the end of the story, when he will wipe every tear from our eyes, Jesus weeps with us when we weep.
- Often, we won't understand the reason for our suffering, but God knows the end of our story and if we are trusting in him it will be unimaginably good.

How Can You Believe in Heaven and Hell?

I've just finished watching a show called *The Good Place*. In the first episode, a woman called Eleanor wakes up in an unfamiliar place. A man tells her, kindly, that she's died. But everything is fine! She lived a really good life on earth, so she's come to the "Good Place." Everyone in the Good Place earned enough points in their lives to deserve super-happy afterlives. Each person gets to live in his or her ideal house, with a specially selected soul mate. They eat their favorite foods and own their perfect pets. They even get to learn to fly!

But Eleanor has a problem. She knows she *isn't* good! In her life on earth, she was selfish, dishonest, and cruel. She's not a murderer or psychopath. She doesn't think she deserves the Bad Place. But she knows there's been a big mistake. Eleanor thinks she should be in a Medium Place, for people who are just okay. And she's afraid she'll get found out.

Many people think of heaven like that. If we're good people, we earn our way to a good place called heaven. Strangely, even people who don't believe in God at all will often talk about loved ones who have died looking down from a "better place." But if there is no God, there is no better place. There's only death. Unlike Eleanor, most people think that if there is a good place, they're probably good enough to go there. And if there's a bad place—a place called hell—that's just for really terrible people, like Hitler and Stalin.

So what does the Bible say about heaven and hell? How can we be sure we'll go to heaven when we die? And if there is a place called hell, how could a loving God send people *there*? This chapter will explore those questions. It's the hardest and most important chapter in this book. It's about the end of the story.

The Real Meaning of Heaven and Hell

In the song "False God," Taylor Swift says her relationship with her boyfriend is like worshiping a false god. Heaven is when they're together. Hell is when they fight. Strange as it may sound, this idea of heaven and hell is closer to what the Bible teaches us than the setup in *The Good Place* show. Because in the Bible, heaven and hell are about our relationship with God. Heaven isn't a place to which God sends us if we're good. Heaven is being in perfect, happy, everlasting relationship with God and with each other. It's Jesus and his people together forever in an unimaginable whole new world. Everything good about God's New Creation—the place where heaven and earth come back together—flows from relationship with him. Hell is the opposite. Hell means facing the judgment of God forever and being shut out of his kingdom.

Taylor Swift sings, "Hell is when I fight with you."[1] According to the Bible, hell is when God fights with us.

You may have heard Christians say that you need to believe in Jesus to go to heaven, and you might have thought, *That's weird! Why would believing in a guy from two thousand years ago make the difference in where you go after you die?* But heaven is all about being with Jesus. At the beginning of *The Good Place*, Eleanor is assigned a soul mate called Chidi. But Jesus says, at the resurrection there will be no human marriage (Matthew 22:30). Why? Because the real marriage—that whole new world of Jesus's marriage to his people that we talked about in chapter 6—will finally have come!

I live with my husband and our three kids. The place I live in isn't just a house, it's a home, and the foundation of our home is my marriage to my husband. If I'd said no to Bryan when he asked me to marry him thirteen years ago, I wouldn't be living with him now. It's like that with Jesus. Taylor Swift made a false god of her relationship with her boyfriend. But there is a true God, who longs for a relationship with her—and with you. He's inviting us to live with him. "I stand at the door and knock," says Jesus. "If anyone hears my voice and opens the door, I will come in to him and eat with him, and he with me" (Revelation 3:20). But if we say no to Jesus now, the day will come when we're longing to get in to his home, but the door will be forever shut.

But you might wonder, is missing out on that relationship with Jesus really so bad?

Is Life without Jesus Really So Bad?

In *Harry Potter and the Prisoner of Azkaban*, we meet the terrible Dementors. Dementors guard the high-security prison of the wizarding world. They don't carry weapons like normal prison guards. Instead, Dementors suck the joy and love and happiness out of a room—or even out of a person—until all that is left is coldness and despair. The ultimate punishment in the wizarding world is a Dementor's kiss.

If we don't know Jesus, it's easy to think that we'll be just fine without him. Plenty of people who don't follow Jesus live pretty happy lives on earth. But if Jesus is who he says he is, then truly being without Jesus is like kissing a Dementor. If Jesus is "the light of the world" (John 8:12), then being without Jesus means living in terrible darkness. If Jesus is "the bread of life" (John 6:35), then being without Jesus means being desperately hungry. If Jesus is "the way" (John 14:6), then being without Jesus means being eternally lost. And if Jesus is "the resurrection and the life" (John 11:25), then being without Jesus means being finally, utterly, everlastingly dead. Jesus isn't a guru or a life coach. He didn't come to make our lives better. He *is* the life. Without him, in the end, there is no life for us at all. So how come people can live in this world right now, rejecting Jesus, and seem to do okay?

Two years ago, we fish-sat Bella Lightning, my daughter Eliza's class fish. We collected Bella from the classroom, and I put her bowl on the floor of the passenger seat in our car. I started to drive home. Very slowly. But after a few minutes, I turned a corner a bit too fast, and the goldfish bowl tipped over, sending Bella—flapping wildly—onto the floormat. I pulled the car over as soon as I could and asked my girls if they had any water. I knew that even a couple of minutes without water would kill this fish. Amazingly, my daughter Miranda—who usually doesn't carry a water bottle—had one that day. It had just enough water for Bella to survive.

Before being dumped on the floormat of our car, Bella didn't know she needed water. She didn't even know she *lived* in water. But as soon as the water was gone, her life became a fast track to death.

Jesus made each one of us and gives us everything we have: our family, our friends, our health, even the air we breathe. We can live a long time without realizing Jesus gave us these things, just like we can live without realizing we're breathing air. We can't see it. We can't hear it. We can't smell it. But if it stopped being there for us, even for a minute, we'd be thrown into sudden, terrifying panic. And after a few minutes, we'd be dead.

God's goodness to us now is like the air we breathe, or like the water in which Bella swims. We take it for granted. But without it, we'd have nothing. And if we reject Jesus in our lives on earth, the Bible warns us that in the end, he will reject us.

But is that fair?

Is God Fair to Judge Us?

At the beginning of the Harry Potter series, we meet Harry's aunt Petunia and uncle Vernon. Throughout Harry's childhood, they're horrible to him. They make him sleep in a cupboard under the stairs. They constantly say and do mean things to him. They wish he didn't exist. When Vernon has important guests over, he tells Harry to stay in his bedroom, make no noise, and pretend he doesn't exist. If Harry (aged one) hadn't defeated Voldemort, Vernon and Petunia would probably be dead. Voldemort would have taken over the world, and his followers would be killing

Muggles like the Dursleys just for fun. But Vernon and Petunia think they're being incredibly kind to let Harry live in their house. They don't think they're bad people. In fact, they think they're really very good.

Most of us like to think we're basically good people. We know we're not perfect. We sometimes do bad things. But at heart, we think we're pretty good. We're not like the murderers we hear about on the news or read about in history books. So the idea that we might one day be judged by God doesn't seem fair. But what if, at heart, we actually *aren't* good?

You know when you're reading a comic book and there's a cloud-shaped bubble over someone's head, showing that character's thoughts? Imagine for a minute that you had one of those bubbles over *your* head in real life. Imagine all your thoughts would ping up there, moment by moment, so anyone could read them. What would people think of you?

Try an experiment between now and this time tomorrow. Notice what you're thinking and imagine other people could see your thoughts. Scary, right? If that happened to me, all my relationships would be ruined—even with the people I really like! It's not that *all* my thoughts are bad. But many of them are. Even when I'm doing something good, I always have some messed up thoughts mixed in. And here's the thing: the Bible tells us God *can* see our thoughts. It's like he has x-ray vision to see right through us, even when we're looking pretty good to other people. And God's standards are *really* high.

In *The Good Place* show, only people who have lived a *really* good life have enough points to get into heaven. But Jesus sets the bar even higher. For example, we might think that murdering someone would be bad enough to deserve God's judgment. But Jesus says that anyone who is angry with someone else deserves God's judgment (Matthew 5:21–22). At first, this sounds crazy. We wouldn't dream of murdering someone! But if you think about it, for most of us, murdering someone else wouldn't make our lives better—quite the opposite. But what if we were in a situation where murdering someone else *would* make our lives better?

There are lots of examples throughout history of people murdering to get something they wanted or because of peer pressure from the people around them. You probably know that Hitler was a really bad person. He was. But if you learn about Nazi Germany, you'll discover that thousands of seemingly normal people—who were probably nice to their families and friends—were willing to join in with the murder of six million Jews. Many of the Nazis didn't think they were bad people. They thought they were patriots.

I'm sure you know that slavery is wrong. But if you learn about the history of slavery in America, you'll discover that thousands of white Americans were willing to keep black people as slaves, and many were willing to beat and abuse their slaves without thinking they themselves were bad people. It's what everyone around them was doing. Few people in my country (Britain) owned slaves personally, but many people made a lot of money from selling enslaved Africans.

We probably think we would have been different if we'd been in Nazi Germany or in Britain or America during the time of slavery. But Jesus, who knows us better than we know ourselves, doesn't think so. If you read his teaching in the Gospels (e.g., Matthew 5:21–48), you'll find that you don't measure up to God's standards—not even close. Like Eleanor, we need to realize that if there's a place called heaven, we don't deserve to be there.

The Bible says that God is perfectly good and holy, and sinful people like me and like you can't be where he is (e.g., Isaiah 6:1–5). It's like when you switch a light on in a room and none of the darkness can stay. So what hope is there for people like us? Should we just try to be better? Or try somehow to hide from God? Or pretend God doesn't exist, because Jesus's standards make us feel bad?

Jesus Is Our Only Hope

In *Harry Potter and the Deathly Hallows*, Harry realizes that part of Voldemort's soul is stored in him. The only way for Voldemort to die is if Harry dies too. Voldemort's evil can't be extracted from Harry any other way. The Bible tells us that we each have sin lodged in us like that piece of Voldemort's soul in Harry. The punishment for sin is death: there's no other way to get it out. But the amazing message of the Bible is that if we put our trust in Jesus, his death on the cross becomes our death. Paul puts it like this: "our old self was crucified with him in order that the body of sin might be brought to nothing, so that we would no longer be enslaved to sin" (Romans 6:6). But if we trust in Jesus, we also get to share his life. That's how Jesus was able to say those wonderful words to Martha: "I am the resurrection and the life. Whoever believes in me, though he die, yet shall he live, and everyone who lives and believes in me shall never die" (John 11:25–26).

Martha didn't deserve eternal, joy-filled life, and nor do we. But Jesus promises that anyone who believes in him will get just that. He's done the dying. He's taken the punishment. He's paid the price. He was the only truly good person who has ever lived. But he took the sins of anyone who would believe in him, so that instead of dying forever suffering God's judgment, we can live forever enjoying God's love.

I wish I could tell you a story to explain this. But people don't write stories in which good characters die for bad ones. I could say it was a bit like when Lily Potter threw herself in front of Harry to protect him from Lord Voldemort. And it *is* a bit like that, because her sacrifice saved Harry's life. But God isn't like Lord Voldemort, and we're not like an innocent baby. It would be more like if Dumbledore had died to save Tom Riddle.

I could say it was a bit like when Anna threw herself between Elsa and Hans to save Elsa from being murdered. And it *is* a bit like that, because—like Jesus—Anna took the hit and the power of her love meant she came back to life again. But really, Jesus dying for us is more like if Anna had sacrificed herself for Hans.

I could say it's a bit like the moment in *Titanic* when Jack decides to give his life for Rose, and freezes to death in the water, because he loves her so much. And it *is* a bit like that, because Jesus loves us desperately. But it would be more like Jack dying for Rose's mean fiancé.

Paul explains the strangeness of the cross like this: "For one will scarcely die for a righteous person, though perhaps for a good person one would dare even to die—but God showed his love for us in that while we were still sinners, Christ died for us" (Romans 5:7–8).

If God is the one who gave us life and breath and everything we have—if he even sent his Son to die for us—and we act like he doesn't exist, we're worse than the Dursleys. We're like a kid whose parents loved him and cared for him and gave him everything, but the kid just acted like his parents weren't there. If then, one day, after years of loving patience and inviting him into relationship, his parents said, "It's time for you to leave," we wouldn't think they were unfair. We'd think that kid deserved it.

Jesus told a story in which a son acted just that way to his father: he took his father's money, left home, and spent his father's cash on having fun. When he ran out of money, he realized how stupid he'd been and how miserable he was. He assumed his father wouldn't want him back as a son, but thought maybe he'd take him back as a servant. But when he came within sight of his father's house, his father ran out to meet him and flung his arms around his son and kissed him. He even threw a big party to celebrate his son's return (Luke 15:11–32). Jesus says God loves us like that. He's not just willing to have us back. He's eager for it, running down the street, hugging us tight and throwing a party to welcome us home. But Jesus is also very clear throughout his teachings that one day it will be too late (e.g., Matthew 25:1–13; Luke 16:19–31). The door will be shut. The windows will be closed. There'll be no way to come home anymore.

What about You?

We all have the chance to put our trust in Jesus. Whatever we've done, whatever we've thought, however we've lived. If we cry out to Jesus, he'll welcome us with open arms. In fact, even when Jesus was hanging on the cross, a criminal who was also being executed admitted that he deserved his punishment and then said, "Jesus, remember me when you come into your kingdom" (Luke 23:42). Jesus replied, "Today, you will be with me in paradise" (Luke

23:43). This man knew he hadn't lived a good life. If there was a good place, he didn't deserve it. But in the real Good Place, Jesus is King, and anyone who trusts in him is welcome. All we have to do is admit that we need him, say we're sorry for the ways we have failed to love God and others, and trust that Jesus died for us.

When we come to Jesus, we find out two things: (1) we are more sinful than we ever thought, and (2) we are more loved than we ever dreamed. The one truly good person who has ever lived knows everything about you. He can read your thought bubbles and has the right to judge you. But he loves you so much he was willing to die for you and take that judgment on himself.

Maybe this all seems offensive to you. Maybe as you examine Christianity, it still looks like Sirius Black before Harry realized he'd been falsely accused. Or maybe you're starting to get interested in Jesus, but you still have questions that haven't been answered in this book. If that's you, it's okay to keep asking questions. I've been a Christian for ages, and I still ask questions. But I make sure I ask hard questions not just about Christianity but also about the alternatives, including atheism. Every time I do, I find that Christianity—crazy as it might sometimes sound—is actually the most believable option.

If that's what you've decided too and you're ready now to put your trust in Jesus, here's a prayer you could pray:

Lord Jesus,
It's amazing that you would die for someone like me. If other people knew my thoughts, they'd run away. But you ran toward me instead. I believe that you are God's own Son and that you died on the cross, so that my sin could be forgiven. I believe

that you rose from the dead, so now I can live with you forever. I believe that you love every inch of me—more than anyone else ever could—and that life with you is the only path to true and lasting happiness. Thank you for promising to love me forever. Please be my King and remember me when you come into your kingdom.

Amen.

What Now?

If you've prayed a prayer like that for the first time, welcome! You've just joined a family of people from all over the world. My friend Rachel first prayed a prayer like that when she was reading a book called *Mere Christianity* by C. S. Lewis in a library. Rachel didn't know any Christians, but she found out that a Christian group at her university was having a Valentine's Day party that same week, so she went along. The people Rachel met at that party helped her live her new life as a Christian. One friend she met that night is still helping her today, sixteen years later!

You see, Christians don't belong by themselves. We need a church family where we can get help and give help to others. Just like on a sports team, all of us are needed! But don't expect the Christians you meet to be perfect. They're not. In fact, they're pretty bad. If you could see the thought bubbles above their heads, you'd likely run away. But Jesus ran toward them, just as he has run toward you. And he's sent his Spirit to live in each of his followers, so we're never alone.

Unlike most captains, Jesus doesn't pick strong people for his team, he picks weaklings. He doesn't pick winners, he picks losers. As Paul puts it, "God chose what is weak in the world to shame the strong" (1 Corinthians 1:27). But Jesus's team will win in the end, because Jesus is the hero. It's a bit like Quidditch in the Harry Potter series. In Quidditch, all the players except the Seeker try to score goals against the other team. Each goal scores ten points. But the Seeker's job is to catch the golden snitch, and that's worth 150 points. The team can be losing really badly. But if the Seeker gets the golden snitch the team still wins.

Often, it feels like Jesus's team is losing. We're a bunch of weaklings after all. But Jesus is our Seeker and the salvation he's won for us is worth all the points in the world. Like the golden snitch from Harry's first Quidditch game, it contains the resurrection stone, and it will open at the close.

"I am the resurrection and the life," says Jesus. "Whoever believes in me, though he die, yet shall he live, and everyone who lives and believes in me shall never die. Do you believe this?" (John 11:25–26).

- Heaven isn't a place you get to go to if you've done enough good things in your life. It's the full experience of relationships with God and with each other.
- None of us deserve this amazing relationship with God. We may think we're good people, but God sees our thoughts and knows our hearts. He's given us everything we have, and we've rejected him.
- If we trust in Jesus now, his death on the cross pays the price for our sin, and we will be welcomed into his kingdom. He is eager for us to come to him and welcomes anyone who will accept his offer.
- If we reject Jesus now, he will one day reject us. Every good thing we have will be gone, and we will be shut out of his kingdom forever.
- If we trust in Jesus now, God lives in us by his Spirit and welcomes us into his family.
- Everyone else in Jesus's family is a sinner like us. But we can help each other as we live for him. And in the end, however much we fail, it's Jesus's victory that will count. He is our resurrection and our life.

A "Thank You" Note

I told you in chapter 1 that I hate writing "thank you" notes. But this is an exception. It brings me joy to thank the people who have helped me write the book that's in your hands.

First, I want to thank Miranda, Eliza, and Luke. They made me want to write this book and gave me lots of laughs and love and hugs along the way. My girls have even started writing themselves. I can't wait to read their grown-up books as well.

Second, I want to thank my running mates. I don't literally run with other people very much. But I have some fellow writer friends who keep me company along the way. They cheer me up when I feel down and read my work when I'm too embarrassed to show it to anyone else. Rachel Gilson read every word of this book before anyone else and helped me believe it wasn't awful. I suppose I could theoretically write without her comradeship, but I hope I never have to. Sam Allberry pepped me up when I was floundering and gave me helpful feedback on chapters 7 and 8. Paul calls his friend Epaphroditus his "brother and fellow worker and fellow soldier" (Philippians 2:25). I can say all those things of my friend Sam.

I'm grateful to everyone at Crossway and The Gospel Coalition who helped with this book. Collin Hansen was once again a trusted adviser and a source of ongoing encouragement. Laura Yiesla was a patient and long-suffering editor, putting up with all my authorial awkwardness, and the whole team at Crossway—including Dave DeWit, Lauren Susanto, and Darcy Ryan—have worked tirelessly to put this book in your hands.

I'm thankful for everyone who read drafts of part (or all) of this book and gave me feedback. Pastor and author Claude Atcho and MIT professor Ian Hutchinson ran their expert eyes over chapters 2 and 6 respectively. A cohort of thoughtful younger readers gave me feedback on early drafts, including Lukas Hoeltje, Grace Rogers, Solomon R.V., Madeleine Irving-Stonebraker, Isaac Jump, Will Jump, Zoë Ford, Sam Cranch, Abby Simmons, Karsen Cain, Elijah Zorn, Katie Willis, Zoe DeBenning, Tim Molokov, Molly Lin, Mabry Orndorff, Sophia Shane, Mira Thorp, Katie VanTil, Char DeKoekkoek, Lydia Poteet, Becky Paynter, and Lex Stokes. Their encouragement helped me to believe I could write for younger minds, and their feedback helped me do so better.

Prayer is vital to any Christian's work, and I'm thankful for all the people who have prayed with me along the way, especially Karolyn Park, Julie Ferrell, and Lexi Miltenberger, who prayed with me weekly and helped me keep my eyes on Jesus.

The opportunities I have today are due in large part to the sacrifices my parents made for me when I was your age. Nicholas and Christine Beale's investment in my education—both inside and outside the home—is a gift I can never repay, but I can still be very thankful for it.

Finally, I want to thank my husband, Bryan. When I was a kid, I thought that marriage made your problems disappear. But I was wrong. Instead, I've discovered that a good marriage gives you a partner in the midst of problems and a picture of the kind of love that Jesus has for us—a love that knows us at our worst and still loves us with an indestructible love. God promises, "I will never leave you nor forsake you" (Hebrews 13:5). I'd bet my life on Bryan sticking with me to the end as well.

If you've stuck with this book to its end, I'm thankful for you too. Perhaps you love Harry Potter like I do. If so, this book may have felt like Harry's first letter from Hogwarts: a strange invitation into an unknown world. If that's you, I hope you'll accept the invitation. Or maybe it felt more like a room of requirement, where you could train as part of Dumbledore's Army. If you're a follower of Jesus, you're not too young to fight for the truth. But never forget: in Jesus's army, we only use weapons of love.

Notes

Note to Parents, Grandparents, Guardians, and Friends

1. Richard Dawkins, *Outgrowing God: A Beginner's Guide* (New York: Random House, 2019), 10.

2. See "The Future of World Religions: Population Growth Projections, 2010–2050," Pew Research Center, April 2, 2015, http://www.pew forum.org/2015/04/02/religious-projections-2010-2050/ and "Projected Change in Global Population, 2015–2060," Pew Research Center, March 31, 2017, http://www.pewforum.org/2017/04/05/the -changing-global-religiouslandscape/pf_17-04-05_projectionsupdate _changepopulation640px/.

3. Chapter 1 will feature some of the evidence for this claim. Atheist psychologist Jonathan Haidt summarizes it like this: "Surveys have long shown that religious believers in the United States are happier, healthier, longer-lived, and more generous to charity and to each other than are secular people. . . . Religious believers give more money than secular folk to secular charities, and to their neighbors. They give more of their time, too, and of their blood." Jonathan Haidt, "Moral Psychology and the Misunderstanding of Religion," *Edge*, September 21, 2007, https://www.edge.org/conversation/jonathan_haidt-moral -psychology-and-the-misunderstanding-of-religion.

4. Dawkins, *Outgrowing God*, 103.

5. Erica Komisar, "Don't Believe in God? Lie to Your Children," *Wall Street Journal*, December 5, 2019, https://www.wsj.com/articles/dont -believe-in-god-lie-to-your-children-11575591658.

6. Ying Chen and Tyler J. VanderWeele, "Associations of Religious Up-bringing with Subsequent Health and Well-Being from Adolescence to Young Adulthood: An Outcome-Wide Analysis," *American Journal of Epidemiology*, 187, no. 11 (November 2018): 2355–364, https://academic.oup.com/aje/article/187/11/2355/5094534.

7. Tyler J. VanderWeele and John Siniff, "Religion's Health Effects Should Make Doubting Parishioners Reconsider Leaving," *USA Today*, March 21, 2019, https://www.usatoday.com/story/opinion/2019/03/21/study-leaving-religion-sex-abuse-scandals-affects-public-health-column/3224575002/. These effects are not limited to youth. Another Harvard study published in 2020 found that women who attend religious services weekly were 68 percent less likely to die "deaths of despair" (i.e., deaths caused by suicide, alcohol, or drug abuse) than those who never attended, while churchgoing men were 33 percent less likely to die such deaths than their secular peers. (See Ying Chen, Howard K. Koh, Ichiro Kawachi, Michael Botticelli, Tyler J. VanderWeele, "Religious Service Attendance and Deaths Related to Drugs, Alcohol, and Suicide among US Health Care Professionals," *JAMA Psychiatry*, May 6, 2020, https://jamanetwork.com/journals/jamapsychiatry/fullarticle/2765488.)

8. Komisar, "Don't Believe in God? Lie to Your Children."

Introduction

1. See "The Future of World Religions: Population Growth Projections, 2010–2050," Pew Research Center, April 2, 2015, http://www.pewforum.org/2015/04/02/religious-projections-2010-2050/ and "Projected Change in Global Population, 2015–2060," Pew Research Center, March 31, 2017, http://www.pewforum.org/2017/04/05/the-changing-global-religiouslandscape/pf_17-04-05_projectionsupdate_changepopulation640px/.

2. See Antonia Blumberg, "China on Track to Become World's Largest Christian Country by 2025, Experts Say," *HuffPost*, April 22, 2014, http://www.huffingtonpost.com/2014/04/22/china-largest-christiancountry_n_5191910.html.

Chapter 1: How Can I Live My Best Life Now?

1. *Moana*, directed by Ron Clements and John Musker (Burbank, CA: Walt Disney Animation Studios, 2016).

2. See Tyler J. VanderWeele and John Siniff, "Religion May Be a Miracle Drug," *USA Today*, October 28, 2016, https://www.usatoday.com /story/opinion/2016/10/28/religion-churchattendance-mortality -column/92676964/.

3. For a detailed literature review on the effect of religious participation on health and well-being, see Tyler J. VanderWeele, "Religion and Health: A Synthesis," in *Spirituality and Religion within the Culture of Medicine: From Evidence to Practice*, ed. Michael J. Balboni and John R. Peteet (New York: Oxford University Press, 2017), 357–401.

4. As Tyler J. VanderWeele puts it, "The effect sizes on all-cause mortality are similar to or only slightly less substantial than those for many other important health exposures such as physical activity, tobacco smoking cessation, the use of beta-blockers for congestive heart failure, screening for mammography, and fruit and vegetable consumption." See VanderWeele, "Religion and Health: A Synthesis," 360–61.

5. See Tyler J. VanderWeele and John Siniff, "Religion's Health Effects Should Make Doubting Parishioners Reconsider Leaving," *USA Today*, March 21, 2019, https://www.usatoday.com/story/opinion/2019/03 /21/study-leaving-religion-sex-abuse-scandals-affects-public-health -column/3224575002/.

6. A study of women in the US found that those who attended religious services once a week or more were five times less likely to kill themselves than those who never went. See Tyler J. VanderWeele, Shanshan Li, Alexander C. Tsai, et al., "Association between Religious Service Attendance and Lower Suicide Rates among US Women," *JAMA Psychiatry*, August 2016, https://jamanetwork.com/journals /jamapsychiatry/article-abstract/2529152.

7. J. K. Rowling, *Harry Potter and the Goblet of Fire* (New York: Scholastic, 2002).

8. *Frozen*, directed by Chris Buck and Jennifer Lee (Burbank, CA: Walt Disney Animation Studios, 2013).

9. See Robert Waldinger, "What Makes a Good Life? Lessons from the Longest Study on Happiness," TEDxBeaconStreet video, November 30, 2015, https://www.youtube.com/watch?v=q-7zAkwAOYg.

10. For a summary of research on the benefits of volunteering, see Caroline E. Jenkinson, et al., "Is Volunteering a Public Health Intervention? A Systematic Review and Metanalysis of the Health and Survival of Volunteers," *BMC Public Health* 13 (2013): 773. For a study on caring for others being more beneficial for the carer than the cared for, see for example, Susan Brown, et al., "Providing Social Support May Be More Beneficial Than Receiving It: Results from a Prospective Study of Mortality," *Psychological Science* 14, no. 4 (2003): 320–27.

11. For a summary of this research, see Arthur Brooks, *Who Really Cares* (New York: Basic Books, 2006), 34.

12. See, for example, Robert A. Emmons and Michael E. McCullough, "Counting Blessings versus Burdens: An Experimental Investigation of Gratitude and Subjective Well-Being in Daily Life," *Journal of Personality and Social Psychology* 84, no. 2 (February 2003): 377–89.

13. For surveys of research, see Loren L. Toussaint, Amy D. Owen, and Alyssa Cheadle, "Forgive to Live: Forgiveness, Health, and Longevity," *Journal of Behavioral Medicine* 35, no. 4 (2012): 375–86; Loren L. Toussaint, Everett L. Worthington, and David R. Williams, eds., *Forgiveness and Health: Scientific Evidence and Theories Relating Forgiveness to Better Health* (Dordrecht: Springer, 2015).

14. For research on this, see Angela Duckworth, *Grit: The Power of Passion and Perseverance* (New York: Scribner, 2016).

15. *Aladdin*, directed by Guy Ritchie (Burbank, CA: Walt Disney Studios, 2019).

16. See, for example, Jonathan Haidt, *The Happiness Hypothesis: Finding Modern Truth in Ancient Wisdom* (New York: Basic Books, 2006), 88–89.

17. For research on this see Haidt, *The Happiness Hypothesis*, 222.

18. Haidt, *The Happiness Hypothesis*, 222.

19. See Professor Hastings's personal statement here: http://web.mit.edu/hastings/www/home.html.

Chapter 2: Isn't Christianity against Diversity?

1. See Frederick Douglass, *The Life and Times of Frederick Douglass* (Radford, VA: Wilder, 2008), 49.

2. Quoted in "Sojourner Truth: Abolitionist and Women's Rights Advocate," *Christianity Today*, September 2018, www.christianitytoday.com.

3. See David Masci, "5 Facts about the Religious Lives of African Americans," Pew Research Center, February 7, 2018, https://www.pewresearch.org/fact-tank/2018/02/07/5-facts-about-the-religious-lives-of-african-americans/.

4. In the US, 68 percent of self-identified atheists are men, and 78 percent are white, compared with 66 percent of the general population. See Michael Lipka, "10 Facts about Atheists," Pew Research Center, December 6, 2019, https://www.pewresearch.org/fact-tank/2019/12/06/10-facts-about-atheists/.

5. See "The Global Religious Landscape," Pew Research Center, December 18, 2012, https://www.pewforum.org/2012/12/18/global-religious-landscape-exec/.

Chapter 3: Can Jesus Be True for You but Not for Me?

1. You can read more of Praveen's story here: http://www.veritas.org/faith-identity-dna/.

2. You can read more of Mark's story here: http://www.veritas.org/surprised-jesus-harvard/.

3. *Titanic*, directed by James Cameron (Los Angeles, CA: Twentieth Century Fox, 1997).

4. *Titanic* (1997).

Chapter 4: Can't We Just Be Good without God?

1. *Wreck-It Ralph*, directed by Rich Moore (Burbank, CA: Walt Disney Animation Studios, 2012).

2. Yuval Noah Harari, *Sapiens: A Brief History of Humankind* (New York: Harper, 2015), 109.

3. Harari, *Sapiens*, 111.

4. For example, in 2012, medical ethicists Alberto Giubilini and Francesca Minerva published a paper in the *Journal of Medical Ethics* arguing that "after-birth abortion (killing a newborn) should be permissible in all cases where abortion is, including cases where the newborn is not disabled." Alberto Giubilini and Francesca Minerva, "After-Birth Abortion: Why Should the Baby Live?," *Journal of Medical Ethics*, 2012: 1, https://jme.bmj.com/content/39/5/261.

5. Selective abortion and infanticide has led to a gender gap of twenty-five million in India and thirty-five million in China. See Elaine Storkey, "Violence against Women Begins in the Womb: Why Female Feticide Threatens the Social Order," *Christianity Today*, May 2, 2018, https:// www.christianitytoday.com/ct/2018/may-web-only/violence-against -women-begins-in-womb-abortion.html.

6. *House M.D.*, season 7, episode 23, "Moving On," directed by Greg Yaitanes, written by Kath Lingenfelter and Peter Blake, aired May 23, 2011, on FOX.

7. This widely reprinted remark about religion at a science conference in April 1999 in Washington, DC, won Weinberg the Freedom from Religion Foundation's "Emperor Has No Clothes Award." Freedom from Religion Foundation, "Emperor Has No Clothes Award: Steven Weinberg—1999," accessed September 14, 2018, https://ffrf.org/outreach /awards/emperor-has-no-clothes-award/item/11907-steven-weinberg.

8. Quoted in Sohrab Behdad and Farhad Nomani, eds., *Islam and the Everyday World: Public Policy Dilemmas, Routledge Political Economy of the Middle East and North Africa* (London: Routledge, 2006), 75.

9. Philosopher Christian Miller observes that "literally hundreds of studies" link religious participation to better moral outcomes. Christian B. Miller, *The Character Gap: How Good Are We?* (Oxford: Oxford University Press, 2018), 239.

10. Richard Dawkins, *River Out of Eden: A Darwinian View of Life* (New York: Basic Books, 1996), 133.

11. *Wreck-It Ralph* (2012).

Chapter 5: How Can You Believe the Bible Is True?

1. *Aladdin*, directed by Guy Ritchie (Burbank, CA: Walt Disney Studios, 2019).

2. Cambridge scholar Peter Williams wrote an excellent book about this called, *Can We Trust the Gospels?* (Wheaton, IL: Crossway, 2018).

3. See Richard Bauckham, *Jesus and the Eyewitnesses: The Gospels as Eyewitness Testimony* (Grand Rapids, MI: Eerdmans, 2008).

4. *The Princess Bride*, directed by Rob Reiner (Beverly Hills, CA: Act III Communications, 1987).

5. Ian Hutchinson, *Can a Scientist Believe in Miracles? An MIT Professor Answers Questions on God and Science* (Downers Grove, IL: Inter-Varsity Press, 2018).

Chapter 6: Hasn't Science Disproved Christianity?

1. *Moana*, directed by Ron Clements and John Musker (Burbank, CA: Walt Disney Animation Studios, 2016).

2. See Hans Halvorson, "Why Methodological Naturalism?" in *The Blackwell Companion to Naturalism*, ed. Kelly James Clark (Chichester, West Sussex, UK: Wiley-Blackwell, 2016).

3. Francis Collins, *The Language of God: A Scientist Presents Evidence for Belief* (New York: Free Press, 2006), 20.

4. See Joan Centrella, "A Passion for Science and a Passion for God," in R. J. Berry, ed., *Real Scientists, Real Faith* (Monarch Books, 2009), 109–97.

5. See David L. Chandler, "In Search of New Ways of Producing Nano-Materials," *MIT News*, May 9, 2012, http://news.mit.edu/2012/profile-kong-0509.

6. See "MIT Professor and Dean Daniel Hastings Shares His Worldview at The Veritas Forum" (video), YouTube, June 28, 2011, https://www.youtube.com/watch?v=OGmNPWsR7_I.

7. Russell Cowburn, "Nanotechnology, Creation and God," TEDxStHelier video, August 27, 2015, https://www.youtube.com/watch?time_continue=3&v=UepCFseK_os.

8. "Those laws are within the grasp of the human mind: God wanted us to recognize them by creating us after his own image so that we could share in his own thoughts." Quoted from a letter from Johannes Kepler to the Bavarian Chancellor Herwart von Hohenburg, April 9/10, 1599, Collected in Carola Baumgardt and Jamie Callan, *Johannes Kepler Life and Letters* (New York: Philosophical Library, 1953), 50.

9. For example, one of Charles Darwin's closest scientific colleagues was a Harvard professor named Asa Gray. Gray was a passionate Christian, and he kept trying to persuade Darwin to trust in Jesus. Today, there are Christians who are leaders in evolutionary science: for example, Cambridge professor Simon Conway Morris, who is a leading expert

on the fossil record of how many different forms of life emerged; Gregory Wray, who is a Professor of Biology at Duke University and an expert in the evolution of gene regulation; and Justin Barrett, who pioneered the field of evolutionary psychology of religion.

10. Stephen Hawking, "'There Is No Heaven; It's a Fairy Story,'" interview by Ian Sample, *The Guardian*, May 15, 2011, https://www.theguardian.com /science/2011/may/15/stephen-hawking-interview-there-is-no-heaven.

11. See Ard Louis, "Science or Religion: Do We Have to Choose?" http:// www-thphys.physics.ox.ac.uk/people/ArdLouis/downloads/Ard-Louis -London-Alpha-Oct10.pdf.

12. Ian Hutchinson, *Can a Scientist Believe in Miracles? An MIT Professor Answers Questions on God and Science* (Downers Grove, IL: InterVarsity Press, 2018), 32.

Chapter 7: Why Can't We Just Agree That Love Is Love?

1. See, for example, Tyree Oredein and Cristine Delnevo, "The Relationship between Multiple Sexual Partners and Mental Health in Adolescent Females," *Community Medicine & Health Education* 3, no. 7 (December 23, 2013): 3:256, https://www.omicsonline.org/the -relationship-between-multiple-sexual-partners-and-mental-health -in-adolescent-females-2161-0711.1000256.php?aid=21466, which found that "the prevalence of sadness, suicide ideation, suicide plans and suicide attempts increased with the number of sexual partners across all racial/ethnic groups"; and Sandhya Ramrakha et al., "The Relationship between Multiple Sex Partners and Anxiety, Depression, and Substance Dependence Disorders: A Cohort Study," *NCBI* 42, no. 5 (July 2013): 863–72, published online February 12, 2013, https://www.ncbi.nlm.nih.gov/pmc/articles/PMC3752789/, which found "a strong association between number of sex partners and later substance disorder, especially for women."

2. See, for example, David G. Blanchflower and Andrew J. Oswald, "Money, Sex and Happiness: An Empirical Study," *The Scandinavian Journal of Economics* 106, no. 3 (2004): 391–602, which found that "The happiness-maximizing number of sexual partners in the previous year is calculated to be 1."

3. One ministry you might contact if you need help is Harvest USA at https://harvestusa.org/.

4. Professor Diamond summarizes her data in a fascinating lecture at Cornell University titled, "Just How Different Are Female and Male Sexual Orientation?" YouTube video, October 17, 2013, https://www.youtube.com/watch?v=m2rTHDOuUBw.

5. See Cornelius Tacitus, *The Annals: The Reign of Tiberius, Claudius, and Nero*, trans. J. C. Yardley (Oxford University Press, 2008), 356.

6. See, for example, Mark H. Butler, Samuel A. Pereyra, Thomas W. Draper, et al., *Pornography Use and Loneliness: A Bidirectional Recursive Model and Pilot Investigation*, PubMed.gov, February 17, 2018, https://pubmed.ncbi.nlm.nih.gov/28448246/.

7. Ministries like covenanteyes.com offer resources to help people who want to stop looking at pornography.

Chapter 8: Who Cares If You're a Boy or a Girl?

1. J. R. R. Tolkien, *The Return of the King* (New York: Ballentine Books, 2012), 114.

2. Tolkien, *The Return of the King*, 114.

3. See Rodney Stark, *The Rise of Christianity: How the Obscure, Marginal Jesus Movement Became the Dominant Religious Force in the Western World in a Few Centuries* (Princeton, NJ: Princeton University Press, 1996).

4. See Michael J. Kruger, *Christianity at the Crossroads: How the Second Century Shaped the Future of the Church* (Downers Grove, IL: IVP Academic, 2018), 36.

5. Kruger, *Christianity at the Crossroads*, 34–35.

6. See "Gender Composition" charts and tables, Pew Research Center, https://www.pewforum.org/religious-landscape-study/gender-composition/ and "The Gender Gap in Religion around the World," Pew Research Center, March 22, 2016, https://www.pewforum.org/2016/03/22/the-gender-gap-in-religion-around-the-world/.

7. Susan Dudley, "Women Who Have Abortions," National Abortion Federation (NAF), revised 2003, http://prochoice.org/wp-content/uploads/women_who_have_abortions.pdf.

8. J. K. Rowling, *Harry Potter and the Philosopher's Stone* (London: Bloomsbury, 1997), 221.

9. See David C. Page, "Every Cell Has a Sex: X and Y and the Future of Health Care," Yale School of Medicine, August 30, 2016, https://medicine.yale.edu/news-article/13321/#:~:text=Humans%20have%20a%20total%20of,X%20and%20one%20Y%20chromosome.

10. There is much controversy over the exact numbers, but it seems that some significant proportion of those who experience gender dysphoria in childhood find that it resolves in adulthood. For example, a study published in 2013 in the *Journal of the American Academy of Child and Adolescent Psychiatry*, followed up with 127 adolescent patients at a gender identity clinic in Amsterdam and found that two-thirds ultimately identified as the gender they were assigned at birth.

Chapter 9: Does God Care When We Hurt?

1. J. K. Rowling, *Harry Potter and the Deathly Hallows* (New York: Scholastic, 2007), 555.

2. J. K. Rowling, *Harry Potter and the Order of the Phoenix* (London: Bloomsbury, 2003), 736.

Chapter 10: How Can You Believe in Heaven and Hell?

1. Taylor Swift, "False God," on *Lover*, Republic Records, August 23, 2019.

General Index

abortion, 72–74, 141, 191n4, 192n5
abundant life, 27–39
abuse, 117, 120
Adam and Eve, 143
adultery, 128
Aladdin (film), 32–33, 36, 83, 118
alcohol, 29, 39, 188n7
Al-Qaeda, 77–78
Aristotle, 101, 102
atheism, 16, 179
  and human rights, 75
  among scientists, 101, 108
"A Whole New World" (song), 118

babies, as property, 69
Barrett, Justin, 194n9
Bauckham, Richard, 85
belief in God, increase of, 22
Bible
  on friendship, 127
  literal reading of, 90–93
  on same-sex marriage, 123–25
  truth of, 83–95
  on women, 138–39

Bible reading, 23
Big Bang theory, 101
biological sex, 151
black church in America, 49–50
Boyle, Robert, 103–4
Buddhists, 57, 59
bullying, 68, 146

Carver, George Washington, 104
Celsus, 139
Centrella, Joan, 104–5
children, as property, 69
China, 22, 80
Christianity, 59
  growth of, 16, 22
  health benefits of, 27–39
  impact on women, 138–42, 153
  most diverse belief system in the world, 50–51, 52
  as misogynistic, 139
Christian life, as difficult, 30–31
Christians, 57, 98
  called to love and befriend transgender people, 148–49, 153

invented modern science, 98–100, 111
as "one body," 127
church family, 180
Collins, Francis, 104
Communism, 79–80, 81
concentration camps, 80
coronavirus, 89
Cowburn, Russell, 105
creation, and science, 97

Darwin, Charles, 106
Dawkins, Richard, 13, 18, 80, 101, 107, 193n9
"deaths of despair," 188n7
depression, 14, 29
Diamond, Lisa, 121
diversity, 41–52
    created by Jesus, 42–43, 47, 50–51
Douglass, Frederick, 50
drugs, 14, 29, 39, 188n7
dying to oneself, 28

Einstein, Albert, 103
elephant and blind villagers story, 56–57
embryo development, 73
equality, invented by Jesus, 45
eunuchs, 145
evolution, and Bible's account of creation, 106–7
execution for faith, 30, 63
eyewitness accounts, 85–86

"False God" (song), 170–71
Faraday, Michael, 103
father love, 114–15

feminism, 139–42
forgiving others, 34–35
freedom, 20
friendship, 127, 131, 133
Frozen (film), 31, 90–91, 113–14, 131, 177

Galileo, 101–3
gender identity, 150, 153, 196n10
Genesis, creation story in, 98
gladiatorial contests, 68
God
    created our bodies, 151, 154
    as faithful husband to his people, 115
    the Father, 114
    as Father to his people, 118
    as good and holy, 176
    is love, 31–32, 114
    judgment of, 174, 175
    love and forgiveness of, 128–29
    steps into our suffering, 162–63
going to church, 28–31, 39
good and evil, 67–81
Good Place (TV show), 169–71, 174–75
good Samaritan, the, 45, 70, 92
gratitude, 33–34
Gray, Asa, 193n9
grit, 35–36

Haidt, Jonathan, 38, 187n3
Halvorson, Hans, 100
happiness, 14–15
Harari, Yuval Noah, 71, 74
Harriet (film), 49–50
Harry Potter and the Deathly Hallows (Rowling), 75–77, 157–58, 164–65, 176

Harry Potter and the Goblet of Fire (Rowling), 30

Harry Potter and the Philosopher's Stone (Rowling), 148

Harry Potter and the Prisoner of Azkaban (Rowling), 19, 24, 171–72

Harry Potter series, 18, 23, 27, 161, 173, 177, 179

Hastings, Daniel, 38

Hawking, Stephen, 108, 110

health benefits
  of Christianity, 27–39
  of religious practice, 14–15

heaven, 170–77, 182

hell, 170

helping others, 32–33

Hindus, 57, 59

Hitchens, Christopher, 28

Hitler, Adolph, 79–80

Holland, Tom, 47, 71, 79

Holy Spirit, 148, 151

House M.D. (TV series), 74

Hoyle, Fred, 101

human beings, as machines, 108–9

human rights, 140
  and atheism, 75
  and Christianity, 71–72, 75

husbands, love for wives, 116

Hutchinson, Ian, 93, 109

hypothesis, 99

Ilesanmi, Oluwole, 55, 58, 60, 61, 62, 63

image of God, 43, 44–45, 48, 74, 98, 106, 108, 114
  as male and female, 136, 151, 153

"in-groups" and "out-groups," 48

infantide, 141, 194n1, 195n5

intersex, 136, 144–45, 153

Irving-Stonebraker, Sarah, 74–75

Islam, 58, 59

Jesus
  befriended Samaritan woman, 45, 70, 138–39
  as the bread of life, 172
  broke through racial and cultural boundaries, 45
  cares about our feelings, 147
  claim to be God, 59–60
  created diversity, 42–43, 47, 50–51
  existence of, 84
  as image of the invisible God, 44, 137–38
  invented equality, 45
  as the light of the world, 172
  love of, 133
  marriage to his church, 116, 118, 171
  as our only hope, 176–78
  as the perfect man, 137–38, 153
  raised from the dead, 87–90, 64, 94
  as the resurrection and the life, 160–61, 165, 172, 176, 181
  on sexual sin, 128
  use of metaphors, 91–92
  was a real person, 94
  wept, 137, 138, 147, 161–62, 166

Jews, 57, 60, 98

Judaism, 57, 58

judgment, 174, 175

Kelvin, Lord, 104
Kepler, Johannes, 105, 193n8
Khoransi, Said Raja'i, 79
King, Martin Luther, Jr., 49, 50
Komisar, Erica, 14, 15
Kong, Jing, 105

Lazarus, 137, 158–64
leadership, 143–44
Lemaître, Georges, 100–1
leprosy, 70
Lewis, C. S., 180
life after death, 110
Lord of the Rings (Tolkien), 27,
   35, 135–36, 152
Louis, Ard, 108
love
   across differences, 45–47
   for enemies, 76
   for God, 45
   of money, 36–37
   for neighbor, 45
   and well-being, 31
"love is love," 113–14, 115, 132
Lydia, 140

male and female, 136–37,
   142–44, 146, 149, 150
marriage
   and happiness, 119
   as picture of Jesus's relationship
      with his people, 125, 132
Mary and Martha, 158, 162
Maxwell, James Clark, 103
men
   called to copy Jesus, 137–38

equality with women, 142–44
Mendel, Gregor, 104
metaphors, 91–92, 118
Miller, Christian, 192n9
misogyny, 139
Moana (film), 27–28, 38, 85, 97,
   110
modern science
   invented by Christians, 98–100
   resisted by Christians, 105–8
moral rules, 67–81
moral teachings of different
   religions, 78–79
Morris, Simon Conway, 193n9
mother love, 114–15
multiple close relationships, 131
Muslims, 57, 58, 78, 80, 98

Nazi Germany, 175
Nero, Emperor, 125
New Atheist movement, 13
New Testament, 23
Newton, Isaac, 103
"nothing buttery," 108–9

Old Testament, 23
"one flesh relationship," marriage
   as, 115–17
one God, 98

parables, 92
Percy Jackson series, 59
Phelps, Michael, 38
Phoebe, 140
Picard, Roz, 93
Pontius Pilate, 84
pornography, 129–30

prayer
  benefits of, 14
  as getting Jesus, 166
  not a vending machine, 161
Princess Bride (film), 88
"pro-choice," 72, 74, 141
prodigal son, 178

racial justice, 20
racism, 20, 48–49, 51, 68, 71
Radcliffe, Daniel, 14–50
relationship with God, 114, 115
religious practice, health benefits
  of, 14–15
"resurrection stone," 164
Rowling, J. K., 18, 149

Samaritan woman, 45, 70,
  138–39
same-sex attraction, 121–26,
  130–31
same-sex friendship, 126–28
same-sex marriage, 20, 123, 124
same-sex sexual relationships,
  125, 132
science, 20
  as amazing, 110
  and creation, 97
"science versus Christianity"
  stories, 102–5, 111
self-control, 36
selfishness, 33
September 11, 2001, terrorist
  attacks, 77–78
Sethupathy, Praveen, 57–58
sex
  as a good gift in marriage, 119,
  132
    outside commitment of mar-
    riage, 74, 119–20, 125, 141
  sexual and romantic love, 115
  sharing the message about Jesus,
  55–64
Shepard, Mark, 57–58
singleness, 126, 132
slavery, 69, 175
slaves, in American history,
  48–49, 52
Stevenson, Bryan, 49
suffering, 158–66
suicide, 29, 39, 188n7, 189n6,
  194n1
Swift, Taylor, 38, 170–71

"them" and "us," 47–49
thought bubble, 174, 180
Tiberius, Emperor, 85
Tice, Rico, 61
Titanic (film), 60–61, 62, 177
Tolkien, J. R. R., 35, 152
transgender people, 145–49, 153
trust in Jesus, 131, 147, 176,
  178–79, 182
truth, 15
  in metaphors, 118
Truth, Sojourner, 50, 140
truth claims of religions, 58–59,
  64
Tryphaena and Tryphosa, 140
Tubman, Harriet, 49–50

unborn babies, as human beings,
  72–74
Universal Declaration of Human
  Rights, 79
universe, birth of, 100

VanderWeele, Tyler J., 14, 22, 28–31, 189n4

Weinberg, Steven, 78–79
Wilberforce, William, 48
wives, submission to husbands, 116–17
woman, as helper, 137

women
  called to copy Jesus, 138
  equality with men, 142–44
  roles of, 142, 153
  work of, 140
women's rights, 140–42
work, value of, 140–41
Wray, Gregory, 194n9
Wreck-It-Ralph (film), 67, 80

Scripture Index

Genesis
1–2 106
1:26–27 43
1:26–28 136
1:27 .... 98, 106
2:15–3:7 143
2:18 137
2:24 .... 115, 117

Deuteronomy
32:6 114

1 Samuel
2:8 102

Psalms
54:4 137
68:5 35
93:1 102
118:7 137

Isaiah
6:1–5 176
49:15 115
53:2 44
53:3 162
54:5–8 116

63:16–17 114

Jeremiah
3:20 116

Ezekiel
16 116

Hosea
1:2 116
11:1–4 114

Matthew
5:21–22 175
5:21–48 175
5:27–28 128
5:43–45 76
6:9 114
7:13–14 92
7:14 36
8:1–4 70
8:3 137
11:28–30 137
12:50 127
16:24 30
16:24–25 148
16:25 32

18:21–22 34
19:3–12 145
19:4 151
19:13–15 70
19:16–26 37
20:16 37
22:30 171
25:1–13 178
26:53 137
28:1–10 89
28:18 60
28:18–20 .... 62, 85
28:19 .... 46, 62

Mark
2:5 60
2:7 60
2:10 60
4:35–41 137
10:13–16 .... 70, 137
10:43–45 144
10:44–45 32
10:45 137
12:29–31 45
12:31 32
14:29–31 87
14:66–72 87
16:1–11 89

Luke
4:40 137
5:31 130
5:34 116
7:36–50 139
8:2–3 140
9:23 28
10:25–37 .... 70, 92
10:38–42 .... 138, 158

11:4 34
15:11–32 178
16:19–31 178
18:15–17 70
22:49–51 137
23:34 .... 35, 76
23:42 178
23:43 178–79
24:1–12 89
24:10–11 143

John
1:1–5 42–43
1:3 147
2:13–17 137
4:1–42 .... 70, 139
4:4–26 45
6:35 .... 91, 172
8:12 172
10:10 28
10:11 91
10:28–29 164
11:3 158
11:5–6 159
11:21–22 160
11:23 160
11:24 160
11:25 .... 60, 62, 137,
                    172
11:25–26 .... 160, 164, 176,
                    181
11:27 162
11:32 162
11:35 .... 137, 162
11:36–37 162
11:39 163
11:43–44 164
13 137

14:6.................56, 58, 60, 172
14:9.................44, 60
14:16.................36
15:5.................91
15:12.................31
15:13.................127
19:11–18...........89
21:9.................137

Acts
2:9–11.................46
2:42.................30
8:26–40.............46, 145
9.................63
16:14.................140
20:35.................32

Romans
1:18–31.............123
3:10–12.............76
5:7–8.................76, 177
5:10.................76
6:6.................176
8:18.................165
8:28.................34, 152, 158
8:35–39.............131
12:5.................127
12:19.................35
16:1.................140
16:1–16.............143
16:12.................140

1 Corinthians
1:27.................181
6:9–10.............123
6:9–11.............125
6:11.................124

7:3–5.................119
7:7.................126
7:32–35.............126
12:27.................46
15:3–4.............58
15:17.................58

2 Corinthians
5:11–14.............63

Galatians
3:28.................142

Ephesians
4:28.................37
5:22–23.............117
5:22–33.............116
5:25.................116, 117
5:28.................117
5:31.................117
5:33.................117

Philippians
1:18.................30
2:1–11.............138
2:18.................30
2:25.................127, 183
3:1.................30
4:2–3.............143
4:4.................30

Colossians
1:15.................44, 137
2:2.................127
3:11.................46
3:16.................30
3:19.................117
3:23.................37

1 Thessalonians
2:7 127
5:16 34
5:18 34

2 Thessalonians
3:12 37

1 Timothy
1:15 63
1:15–16 125
1:8–11 125
2:11–14 143
6:10 37

Philemon
12 127

Hebrews
12:1–2 36

13:5 185

1 Peter
3:7 117
3:15 63

2 Peter
1:6 36

1 John
3:16 .... 31, 131
4:8 .... 31, 114

Revelation
3:20 171
7:9 51
19:7 118
21:1–5 118
21:4 .... 160, 163